T0248547

# GHOSTS AND LEGENDS OF LAFAYETTE AND LOUISVILLE

## DOUG CONARROE

Haunted America

Published by Haunted America
A Division of The History Press
Charleston, SC
www.historypress.com

Copyright © 2023 by Doug Conarroe
All rights reserved

*Front cover*: photo by the author.
*Back cover, top*: Lafayette History Museum, Lafayette Historical Society; *bottom*: Louisville Historical Museum.

First published 2023

Manufactured in the United States

ISBN 9781467152730

Library of Congress Control Number: 2023937180

*Notice*: The information in this book is true and complete to the best of our knowledge. It is offered without guarantee on the part of the author or The History Press. The author and The History Press disclaim all liability in connection with the use of this book.

All rights reserved. No part of this book may be reproduced or transmitted in any form whatsoever without prior written permission from the publisher except in the case of brief quotations embodied in critical articles and reviews.

# CONTENTS

# 1

# EVERYONE LOVES
# A GOOD GHOST STORY

T he first recorded ghost tale in east Boulder County dates to March 15, 1893, when a Lafayette correspondent for the *Boulder Herald* reported that "a little girl saw a small woman dressed in black pass up from the R.R. [railroad] bridge toward the house. As it was nearly dark, the child thought the woman went into the house and passed up the stairs. As the woman could not be found, and was not seen to come down the stairs, there was a mystery about it. Somebody or something may have been seen afterward, but I cannot find that there was."

After reading that a ghost was in their midst, residents reportedly trekked to the site, likely a home east of Lafayette along Coal Creek, to confirm the girl's story. The location is where several railroad bridges traversed the creek for access to the coal mines, an area later platted as the town of Irvington. The Standard coal mine and its scattered miner's cottages occupied Blue Ribbon Hill on the east side of the creek.

A week later, the March 22, 1893 *Boulder Herald* reported that the mysterious sighting had been solved. The ghostly woman in black was a man in a dress who wanted to scare the residents from the house. He'd apparently "entered the unlocked door and began to shake the bed on which the man of the house was lying and the would be sleeper managed to grasp a very substantial hand…and all fears of the supernatural herewith departed."

Lafayette was founded by Mary E. Miller, who platted original Old Town in 1888. She had secured considerable wealth from leasing the coal under her farm to John H. Simpson, who sank the town's first coal mine, the Simpson. In 1927, early pioneer George Bermont, for whom is named Bermont Avenue in Lafayette, said that in 1890 the town had half a dozen houses, a lighting system consisting of coal oil lamps, one mercantile—the Lockwood Trading Company where he worked—and one livery stable. By comparison, Louisville is rooted in 1870s railroad companies needing coal and water for their locomotives. Railroad employee Louis Nawatny was tasked with surveying the railroad's land holdings and sinking the town's first coal mine. He later platted the town site and named it after himself.

# Myths and Legends

In the opening scenes of the 1990s television series *The X-Files*, Agent Dana Scully's boss asks her if she knows about the government's secret stash of documents detailing sightings of monsters, demons and ghosts. "I believe they have to do with unexplained phenomena," says Scully. To which her boss responds, "We trust you'll make the proper scientific analysis."

Elements of folklore and eyewitness accounts of the paranormal have been handed down in writing and in oral traditions since the beginning of civilization. Centuries ago, much of the world—and the universe—was mystical and ethereal, and explanations were simply a matter of lack of understanding. There was no science or scientific method to explain the natural world. The rising and setting sun was as mysterious and unexplained as the folklore surrounding humans who could morph into werewolves.

With the passage of time, myths and legends imbedded in cultures around the world became fewer in number. Humans began to understand the universe and the sun and the moon. But other myths and legends carried through into modern times, only to be glorified and glamorized by Hollywood.

But one element remains true. Experiencing the unexplained is usually confined to one person or a small group of people who retell the encounter in an anecdotal manner. The experience is consequential to the individual in many respects, but the account is still anecdotal. By human nature, the story is passed from person to person and enhanced for better effect. And on and on, to the point that any encounter told by anyone develops and morphs into whatever form a subsequent storyteller desires.

Speaking of a legend that evolved according to the whims of the storyteller, the bulk of this book deals with the legend of the Lafayette Vampire, which has gained national attention and status. Visitors from all over the country visit the alleged vampire's grave site.

My point in writing this book is to concentrate on the origins of local ghost stories, myths and legends and reveal new aspects of the same via eyewitness accounts. There's also an ample dose of debunking, not due to skepticism of ghosts or paranormal activity but in order to accurately tell the history of east Boulder County communities. The "It is said…" aspect of such tales has to be backed up with historical fact, retold by real people who are identified sources. Ghost hunters can do all kinds of "scientific analysis" and retell or make up ghosts tales as they please, but they're not going to make up historical details to go along with them. Not here, anyway.

# THE LAY OF THE LAND

In east Boulder County, more ghost stories are centered in Lafayette than in Louisville or Erie. All of these communities sit on top of former coal mines, the toils of which fueled Denver's factories during the early twentieth century, with the last coal mines near Erie closing in the 1970s. One of the most dangerous vocations on record, coal mining claimed the lives of dozens of local men. As a general rule, most of the bodies made it back to the surface for proper burials. One exception was driver boss (mule driver) Joe Jaramillo, one of eight miners killed in a January 1936 explosion at the Monarch coal mine south of Louisville. Jaramillo's body was never recovered.

With so many lives lost 250 feet underground, the natural conclusion is that there's got to be a lost soul or two among the lot.

On January 18, 1901, the *Lafayette News* reported on the front page that five hundred coal miners went on strike at the Winters Quarters, a haunted coal mine in Schofield, Utah. The "forty or fifty men who quit work… profess to believe that they have at different times seen a headless miner in the workings." The article stated that the ghost was believed to be the spirit of Sandy McGovern, who was killed along with two hundred other men working at the mine six months earlier.

Surprisingly, local ghost tales, sightings and hauntings involving deceased local coal miners are few and far between.

One account of a ghostly underground sighting involves coal miner Chelmar "Shine" Miller, who recounted in a 1984 oral history interview the January 30, 1940 death of fellow miner Jim Sherratt at the Washington

An unidentified coal miner at the Columbine Mine east of Lafayette in about 1942, a few years before the mine closed. Twenty-two men died at the Columbine from 1920 to 1946, and the mine produced over seven million tons of coal. *In the author's collection and from the Rocky Mountain Fuel Company archives at the Denver Public Library, Western History Collection.*

Mine, four miles east of Erie. The mine, run by the Clayton Coal Company, closed in 1967. Miller was a mule driver at the mine and explained that there was a water slip, which was a soapstone formation cutting through the coal seam. This meant that the roof of the area being worked by the two miners was unstable and required lots of timbering to support it.

Miller and Sherratt were working side by side in the entryway when the soapstone roof collapsed, burying Sherratt and partially burying Miller, who was able to escape with minor injuries. Sherratt was not as fortunate and was buried under feet of heavy soapstone. When fellow workers came to help the two, rescuers said they were glad Sherratt was OK and had made it to safety, stating, "We saw Jim a runnin' by" and up the passageway.

Unfortunately, Miller explained to the rescuers, Sherratt wasn't in any condition to run anywhere. He was deceased, buried nearby under tons of rock.

Early Lafayette-area coal miners consisted primarily of immigrants from Wales, the site of the ancient legend of the two-foot-tall Tommyknocker, a leprechaun-like troublemaker who inhabited coal mines. Collapsing ceilings and timbers in areas being mined sometimes knocked prior to collapse,

The mythical Tommyknockers, mischievous elf-like creatures that signaled to coal miners of collapsing ceilings and support timbers. *From* Traditions and Hearthside Stories of West Cornwall *by William Bottrell, illustrated by Joseph Blight, 1873.*

and Cornish and Welsh miners attributed the knocks to Tommyknockers signaling danger.

There's no documentation showing that local coal miners believed in or retold the tale of the Tommyknockers. No such spirit has been attributed to saving the life of a local miner, and none of the dozen or so former east Boulder County miners interviewed for oral histories in the 1970s and '80s mention the pint-sized supernatural beings.

Local miners do mention an age-old superstition that a woman visiting a coal mine is bad luck. Coal miner Jack Davies, interviewed by Rachel Homer in 1978, said that he and fellow miners at the Columbine Mine didn't appreciate women visiting underground sections of the mine. "Every time a woman goes down [into the mine], there's a death," said Davies.

## PLENTY OF TRAGEDIES TO GO AROUND

Unhappy spirits are often rooted in a soul that's not ready to depart and that came about through a tragic death: a love triangle gone bad; a car accident in which a teenage life is cut short; children lost to diphtheria or flu.

Horrible and unimaginable tragedies abound in east Boulder County history, recounted in records of investigations made by the Boulder County coroner.

At the top of the list is thirty-five-year-old Emma E. Nelson, who lived about three miles west of Lafayette, near the intersection of Cherryvale and Arapahoe Roads. In 1916, Emma hanged two of her children, strangled a third, shot her oldest daughter in the back and then turned the revolver on herself. She spared two of her children by sending them to a neighbor's house. So distraught was her husband, William, that a few months later he sold the farm and moved.

There have been other tragedies as well.

In 1905, seven-year-old Jane Williams was hit and killed by a train on the railroad bridge south of Louisville. Several of her friends were injured.

Vincent Domenico, age three, who lived on the Domenico Farm in Lafayette on Baseline Road, died in 1917 after choking on a candy jawbreaker.

In 1944, teenagers James Abeyta, John Espinoza and Charles Munoz were killed on East Baseline Road when their automobile struck a freight train stopped on a siding that crossed the road. A welding crew had to cut apart the car to retrieve the bodies.

Given 150 years of Lafayette, Louisville and Erie history, hauntings and apparitions related to these deaths and others just as tragic are either nonexistent or few and far between—just like hauntings of former coal miners.

But Erie tops the list in terms of strange memorial services. In 1999, the ashes of former Erie City administrator Leon Wurl were mixed into the first load of asphalt applied to Erie's old town streets.

## My Own Experiences

Despite reports of alien abductions occurring in my own Lafayette neighborhood (perhaps the topic of another book?), things have been relatively quiet.

In a 1990s column I wrote for my family's *Louisville Times* and *Lafayette News* newspapers, I talked about the historic Lafayette homes that I've renovated over the years. The 1890s home that my wife and I moved into and then renovated in 1995 was built by Anna Waneka Thomas, the daughter of the area's first European settlers, Adolf and Annie Waneka. Adolf and Annie brought Anna to the new land about 1860. During renovation and even years later, friends asked if there were any ghostly inhabitants, but the house emanated nothing but warm, positive vibes—no apparitions, no mysterious footsteps and no doors mysteriously opening and closing.

I would often reply that if there were otherworldly inhabitants, they'd have to be pretty glad they occupied a nicely renovated and insulated structure, not haunting buried rubble at the landfill.

But a renovation project in a historic fix-and-flip on Elm Street was different. After about a month of demolishing and reassembling the interior, I'd taken a break one summer day to get a haircut—a buzz cut—at the local barber. Returning a few hours later to the jobsite, I had a repeated experience of a hand brushing across the top of my head, assessing the close-cropped hair sticking up. I brushed it off as cobwebs hanging from the ceiling, but the same thing happened in different rooms with nothing present above my head except the nine-foot ceiling.

The common element that surfaces in my rudimentary examination of the paranormal in east Boulder County is change. That is, whenever disruption occurs—an interior or exterior remodeling, for example—once-quiet spirits become active. Very few of the encounters I detail have been considered scary, but it's pretty clear that someone, somewhere, doesn't appreciate change.

# 2

# THE LAFAYETTE VAMPIRE

No sense putting it off or saving the best for last. Without question, east Boulder County's most publicized and long-standing legend is that of the Lafayette Vampire. He's Glava the Vampire, historically known as Fodor the Vampire, and is said to be buried in the Lafayette Cemetery.

The longtime legend boils down to this: A coal miner from Transylvania who was living in Lafayette died in 1918 and was buried in the Lafayette Cemetery. To make sure he didn't rise from the grave, locals dug him up and drove a wood stake through his heart. From the stake grew a tree, which can be seen in the middle of his grave site. Later enhancements to the legend include a rosebush near the grave marker sprouting from the vampire's fingernails and local children seeing a tall, thin man with long fingernails sitting on the grave. The headstone at the site identifies two people, "Tranditor" and "Todor Glava," both Romanians.

True to most legends, the vampire myth has evolved and taken on narratives that are hard to believe. But by the late 2010s, the legend had grown to cult status. Unfortunately, the "enhancements" to the legend make a person want to scream, "C'mon, folks, let's at least get the 'facts' behind the legend correct. Never mind that vampires don't exist!"

As mentioned in the previous chapter, this legend—like all others—has been subject to the inventions and whims of storytellers. The key phrases that are a part of this (and any) unfounded and fabricated tale of terror and mystery are: "my friend says," "some believe," "folks say," "it is said," "as lore has it," "there are reports," "the word was," "legend has it" and "locals say."

The grave site and headstone in the Lafayette Cemetery of Teodor Glava, the Romanian immigrant who is the subject of the Lafayette Vampire legend. The juniper tree that allegedly sprouted from a stake to his heart is visible at the left. *Photo by the author, 2023.*

And the greatest irony is that "locals," as in Lafayette residents who'd heard the legend for decades, scratch their heads about how this legend reached statewide, if not nationwide, cult status. Visitors from all over the country visit Glava's grave all seasons of the year and leave mementos. Room keys, personal notes, sunglasses, costume jewelry, plastic and real flowers, toy vampires and coins. Lots of coins. (Coins left on headstones are a sign of respect. But in this case, respect for the person or respect for the vampire?)

The cult status of the Lafayette Vampire has grown to the point that dirt from Glava's grave site was offered up for auction on eBay. Really. No one knows if the dirt really came from the site; however, city officials were notified of the posting, and eventually eBay took it down.

In reality, the story of Teodor Glava, a Romanian coal miner who immigrated to the United States around 1914, starts in his hometown of Lesnic, Romania, a mining community in the Transylvania region of the Austro-Hungarian empire. Born in 1877, Teodor probably worked in the marble quarries near his Lesnic residence. Hoping to find a better life in America, he left his wife, Sofia, and daughter, Victoria, in Lesnic and landed first in Gary, West Virginia, then Canfield, Colorado, west of Erie. (Estate records show that Glava worked in Lafayette but lived in Canfield.

Trinkets, coins and flowers left at Teodor Glava's grave site. *Photo by the author, 2023.*

Technically, the legend should be called the "Canfield Vampire.") Teodor died in 1918, probably in Canfield, a victim of the flu pandemic. He's buried in the pauper's section of the Lafayette Cemetery, and his grave is marked by a primitive marker made of concrete, with lettering scratched with the pointed end of a brick trowel.

In explaining the vampire legend, we also need to tell the story of the man buried next to Glava and sharing the grave marker: John Trandafir. He and Glava were fellow Romanian immigrants whose hometowns were a few hundred miles apart. Both worked at the Simpson coal mine in Lafayette and were most likely friends.

First, some bookkeeping.

For consistency, the long-buried man brought into indissoluble local lore will be referred to as "Teodor Glava," because that's how he signed his name on his September 12, 1918 military draft registration card. (There are many variations, possibly due to a language barrier, but that's how he signed his name.) Variations of his name include the following:

Toader Glava. June 13, 1914. Ellis Island immigration ledger. Romanian immigrant Petru Dinis lists Toader Glava as a cousin, address Box 106, Gary, West Virginia.

*Teodor Glava*

Tudor Glavor. May 17, 1918. War bond purchase acknowledgement of Simpson Mine employees in *Lafayette Leader*.

Theodore Glava. September 12, 1918. Name put on draft registration card by registrar John Green.

Teodor Glava. September 12, 1918. Glava's own signature on draft registration card.

Theodore Glava. December 6, 1918. Death notice in *Lafayette Leader*.

Toder Glaver. December 12, 1918. Adjustment Day public notice in *Lafayette Leader*.

Toder Glaver. June 4, 1920. Final estate settlement notice in *Lafayette Leader*.

Toder Glaver. All of his estate paperwork on file at the Colorado State Archives in Denver.

Todor Glava. Lafayette Cemetery grave marker; for some reason, the "T" has been interpreted as an "F," hence Fodor Glava.

## How the Legend Started

After two years of my research and conversing with dozens of third- and fourth-generation Lafayette residents, the earliest mention of the vampire in the cemetery comes from Eleanor (Sanchez) Montour, who recalled that when she was a child in the late 1940s and early 1950s, her mom, Alicia Sanchez, occasionally warned her about the Transylvanian in the cemetery and that she should "get home before sundown so that the vampire doesn't get you." Montour acknowledged in 2022 that it was more of a scare or behavior modification tactic designed to keep her from misbehaving. And it worked.

All of the longtime residents interviewed, which covers Lafayette history starting in the 1940s, knew the vampire legend. The premise of a Transylvanian buried in the cemetery was followed by "he's a vampire" in the 1950s, then by the "tree must be the stake in his heart" in the 1960s, followed by the "rosebush is from his fingernails/hair" in the 1970s. Then it became the mysterious man sitting on the headstone or walking in the cemetery in the 1990s, followed by a half dozen other variations leading up to the publication date of this book.

None of the older residents I interviewed ever heard of or saw anything ghostly or ghoulish in the cemetery or at Teodor Glava's grave site. None of the former city employees interviewed for the book who worked in the cemetery experienced anything out of the ordinary. One former police chief, as reported in the newspaper, played up the legend; another, interviewed by me in 2023, didn't pay any attention to it.

No lifelong residents were able to pinpoint the exact time frame for the part of the tale involving the wood stake turning into a tree. That seems to have originated in the late 1950s or early 1960s, when the Christopher Lee vampire movies started hitting the regional drive-in theaters. And none of the older residents could recall hearing (as children) the narrative of a mob of Lafayette residents digging up the grave and staking Glava.

For locals, the early legend was simple: A dude from Transylvania was buried in the cemetery, and Transylvania is where vampires come from.

For decades, schoolkids did share scary cemetery stories on the school playground located about a block east of the cemetery. (The primary and secondary schools were side by side in two buildings on East Baseline Road until 1963, when Lafayette Elementary opened.) For years, the lighted high school football field was located in the former City Park, where the Bob Burger Recreation Center sits. The field was oriented north–south, and the bleachers backed to the cemetery. To avoid the fifteen- or twenty-five-cent entry price, kids often snuck into the games via the cemetery.

Old-timer Beverly (Abeyta) Smith remembers her own nighttime visit to the cemetery in the late 1950s.

"I was in the 8th grade or thereabouts, and my cousin told me and my friends that we could sneak into the football game through the cemetery. So we tried it," said Smith "It was sure spooky walking through there at night, and not particularly because the vampire was supposed to be there, but because it was just a scary place for a kid. As we walked in the dark up this little hill approaching the bleachers these hands reached up and grabbed us and pulled us down. Scared us enough to make us scream out loud. But it was just my cousin and his friends playing a prank.

"My mom had always given me money to get in the game, so I didn't need to sneak in. From that point on I always used it and paid to get it."

Nannette (Summers) Iatesta, another longtime resident who graduated from Lafayette High School in the late 1960s, said in a 2021 interview with the author that "the vampire was not on our radar screens. We loved darting in and out of the [Lafayette and Louisville] cemeteries but no one was really aware of Glava by name. The grave site was practically covered over with wild yellow roses, which [years later] made the whole Transylvania/vampire aspect attractive."

As a student at Centaurus High School in the 1970s, I heard the vampire tale as well. Friends of mine who visited the grave site at night in the 1970s and '80s to drink beer swear they didn't experience anything more than a buzz from the beer.

## THE LEGEND GETS SOME PR

The first published account of a "Transylvanian vampire" is found in the October 31, 1987 *Loveland Reporter-Herald*, describing a grave site in Lafayette Cemetery wherein "the word 'Transylvania' is scratched into the grave's ruddy concrete headstone, and a scraggly pine tree shoots up through the plot's center, an uncanny reminder of the wooden stake through the heart that doomed Dracula.

"'Several years ago we found a doll with a pin stuck through its heart that someone had placed on the grave,' said former police chief Larry Stallcup, who said he learned of the grave site in high school [in the early 1950s]. 'I read it was a voodoo tradition to prevent the buried person from rising from the grave.'"

Edward D. "Jake" Wells, who at the time was a longtime Lafayette resident who placed headstones in the Lafayette Cemetery and at cemeteries along the Front Range, said in the story, "Go up there at midnight and you'll see the vampire sitting right on top of the stone."

The story also paraphrases former Lafayette city clerk Bev Smith, who said that a man named "Tudor Glava" purchased the grave site in 1918 but also that there is "no record of who, in fact, is buried there."

The article continues: "Longmont psychic Dori Spence recently visited the grave site and said she sensed a protective curtain of energy surrounding the grave. 'I definitely sense that a woman is buried there. It feels as if a man buried his housekeeper, or lover, thinking he would be buried here when he died. Later, he may have planted a rose bush before he went back to Transylvania. There is no evil associated with this person. Just the feeling that the grave is some sort of a loose end for both the man and the woman.'"

Then came *Broomfield Enterprise* columnist Shawn Stark, who in the October 29, 1992 edition details "a flat, square stone surrounded by a thick-stemmed rose bush, the telltale inscription: 'Fodor Glava. Born in Transilvania, Austor-Ungaria. Died December 1918.'"

Stark tells the legend of the tree growing from "the center of the grave" and that "folks in Lafayette say the tree grew from a wooden stake driven through the heart of poor Mr. Glava."

Next in line for official accounts of the vampire tale is the *Rocky Mountain News*, which on October 21, 1993, wrote about alleged vampire "Fodor Glava." The story describes a thirteen-year-old student at Angevine Middle School who said "this kid at school" saw the vampire "standing by the bushes near his grave. He had a black suit and long, sharp fingernails."

News reporter Alan Dumas's masterpiece continues: "Growing from the middle of the grave is a tree. They [locals] say a wooden stake was driven through Glava's heart, and it took root in the vampire's blood and grew. Surrounding the grave is a huge rose bush that blooms blood-red in spring. It's said the thorny tangles of this bush are his hair, which still grows as he lies undead underground. The writing on the stone [at his grave] was drawn hastily with a stick. Some say the undead Glava wrote it himself with his fingernail."

An October 1993 color photograph accompanying the *News* article shows the west edge of Glava's grave site and the large nonflowering rosebush, which completely encapsulates and obscures the headstone. Because it is late

A 1993 *Rocky Mountain News* photo of the rosebush that engulfed Teodor Glava gravesite. The caption reads, "Overall of the gravesite in Lafayette Cemetery where a vampire was supposedly buried in 1918." *Photo by Jay Koelzer, from the Denver Public Library, Western History Collection, WH2129.*

fall, there's no foliage on the bush. The photographer notes on the back of the archived photograph that he had to fold back several branches to access and photograph the headstone. (This means that no one could stand or sit on the headstone.)

Wanting to tap into local vampire expertise, the story quotes a nineteen-year-old "knowledgeable amateur folklorist and vampirologist" who worked at Lafayette's Sonic Drive-In and who stated that he gathered knowledge about Glava from "old ladies who live over in the old part of town." He continued: "The story goes that he moved here from Transylvania with his wife, but was bitten by a wolf or something, and it turned him into a vampire. He killed his wife, and a neighbor buried her and cornered him in a barn and drove a stake through his heart. A tree always grows from a vampire stake. It's what keeps him in the ground. They say that when there's a full moon his soul will rise and wander around."

On October 28, 1998, Boulder *Daily Camera* staff writer Margie McAllister wrote about "Boulder County's reputed vampire."

"Lafayette historian Beth Hutchison remembers hearing about Glava [the vampire] back in the 1950s when she was going to Lafayette High School," reads the article. There is mention of the blood-red rosebush/fingernail legend in the article, but this is quelled: "Cemetery workers trimmed the yellow rose bush this summer, says Parks Director Rod Tarullo, who considers the tale 'a good story.'" The article continues: "Last week, Beth Hutchison and her husband, Jim, researched Lafayette Cemetery records and maps, trying to discover if one or two people are buried in the plot. 'Their names are not on any record,' Jim Hutchison said."

Next in line in terms of publicizing the Lafayette Vampire was my weekly *Lafayette News* column Doug's Desk dated October 31, 1998, which stated, "As lore has it, the tree [at the gravesite] sprouted from the stake driven into the heart of the vampire." The column was discussing the roots of Halloween, which was a celebration of life centuries ago.

Then came historian Jim Hutchison's summation of the year 1979 in the book *Lafayette, Colorado History: Treeless Plain to Thriving City*. Published in 1990 by the Lafayette Historical Society, the book recounts the city's history chronologically, and the singular item referenced for the year 1979 is "young people" interpreting the tree coming out of the grave of Transylvanian "Fodor Glava" as a tree growing from the stake driven into the vampire's heart.

"There's a spiny rose bush that's supposed to be blood red when in bloom and…there are tales of sightings at night when the vampire comes out with its blood-red eyes shining," wrote Hutchison.

It's important to note Hutchison's timing of the vampire legend; it doesn't become prominent (or revealed publicly) until 1979. Had it been a part of Lafayette's early history (circa 1918), talked about by early residents or even semi-popular in the 1920s, '30s, '40s, '50s and '60s, Hutchison would have known it and noted it in the book's historical timeline.

Twenty years after *Lafayette, Colorado History* was published, a written account of a 2009 visit to the vampire grave site appears in the Kansas-based Bukovina Society of the America's newsletter, easily found on the internet. The article concentrates on Bukovina, Romania immigrant John Trandafir, whose name is also inscribed on the Glava headstone, but the narrator states, "Lafayette children will dare each other to sit on the headstone at midnight, and they will swear that they saw the vampire in his black suit, as local children have for generations."

Starting about 2010, the legend of the Lafayette Vampire began to gain steam in the online realm. "Enhancements" to the legend popped up on their own without attribution. Made-up facts were linked from one blog post to the next, to the point where it's difficult to track the origins of some "facts."

For posterity, here are the online versions—from bulletin boards, blogs and comment sections—of the tale of the Lafayette Vampire as of 2022, listed in chronological order:

"LAFAYETTE, COLORADO: VAMPIRE GRAVE," ROADSIDEAMERICA.COM
BY SEVERIN SCHNEIDER
WWW.ROADSIDEAMERICA.COM
JUNE 14, 2001

The legend: Two huge, unkempt rosebushes shroud the grave of an eastern European man. The legend says that the rose bushes are the vampire's fingernails and that a tree sprouted from the stake used to slay the vampire.

"INVESTIGATION 114: LAFAYETTE CEMETERY: THE VAMPIRE GRAVE," ANAM
    PARANORMAL, TOPEKA, KANSAS
WWW.ANAMPARANORMAL.COM
NO DATE SHOWN, BUT PROBABLY 2003 OR 2004

The legend states that local kids dared one another to stand near the grave and that many have reported seeing Fodor the vampire—tall and thin, wearing a black coat and with long fingernails. A tree grows from the middle of the grave, where his heart would have been. A thorny red rosebush grows from his fingernails. "That's the story that was told to us."

The Lafayette Cemetery where "Fodor Glava" is buried is a paupers' graveyard, where "poor, diseased or unloved were buried." This narrative states that the plot of ground was purchased by Fodor Glava, but no records indicate who was actually buried there. Glava died in December 1918 at the height of the Spanish flu pandemic that had "the whole town quarantined." His is the only stone remaining in the "old paupers graveyard." References are made to newspaper clippings in which a former Lafayette police chief is reported to have found a doll on the gravestone with pins stuck in it. The chief attributed it to voodoo tradition to prevent those buried from rising from the grave. The investigator's collection of newspaper clippings also reference an unidentified man who set headstones in the cemetery and said, "Go up there at midnight and you'll see the vampires [plural] sitting right on top of the stone." The investigation further states: "According to the local police, people walking through alone get beaten up. When they show up, there is no one around, and the footprints lead back to that grave."

The investigators found that the temperature of the grave marker varied, from "minus 13 all the way up to 102 degrees," but discredited or discounted the "people getting beat up" aspect.

"If Mr. Glava is truly the body under the stone, then he was no vampire! Unless he's one of those really nice, never bites anyone, kind of vampires. We all got a sense of sadness and slight annoyance though. As if the spirit whose body is actually under there is a bit peeved at the assumption that he/she is a vampire. While we were walking about doing the photography, a girl on the sidewalk went past and almost passed out at a camera flash. The danger of scaring someone while investigating this one is high. The vampire rumors are just too much and plentiful there, and it's right off the street where a lot of people can see the dark trees and stones, until your flash goes off, and then they pass out."

"LAFAYETTE, COLORADO: VAMPIRE GRAVE," ROADSIDEAMERICA.COM
BY DREA PENNDRAGON
WWW.ROADSIDEAMERICA.COM
APRIL 10, 2004

The legend: A grave in the Lafayette Cemetery is said to contain a vampire. Young boys dare one another to run into the depths of the cemetery and touch the stone of the vampire.

"Over the last two years, our [paranormal] team has collected over 100 paranormal photographs, as well as many EVP (electric voice phenomena) recordings. One of these EVP recordings, taken right by the vampire grave, clearly asks, 'Do you want my stake?.' [A thermometer also shows] cold spots reaching as low as negative 47 degrees on a night that was otherwise rather mild."

"VAMPIRE GRAVE, LAFAYETTE, COLORADO," WAYMARKING.COM

The legend: For nearly ninety years, locals have been daring one another to stand near the vampire's grave, and a good number of them have seen a tall, thin man with a black coat sitting on top of the stone. The persistent myth is that a tree grew from the stake that killed him. Because cemetery records are so scant, it's difficult to determine if the vampire, "Fodor Glava," is even buried in the cemetery plot he purchased, or that he was even a vampire.

Hundreds of destitute persons were buried in the paupers' area during the 1918 Spanish flu pandemic. "His is the only one with an actual marker, as for the writing on the marker, it is shaky and crude as if scratched in haste, but does that mean he was a vampire? We'll let you decide."

(According to the blog post, the narrative is excerpted from the book *Colorado Curiosities* by Pam Grout, published in 2006.)

*GLAVA*, VAMPIRE-THEMED SILENT MOVIE SHOT ON LOCATION IN LAFAYETTE
  AND BOULDER
DIRECTED BY NICHOLAS BERNHARD, PRODUCED BY NDH FILMS
WWW.YOUTUBE.COM
2010; RERELEASED IN 2015

The storyline: The 1918 Spanish flu epidemic sweeps though Lafayette, leaving mass graves full of immigrants. Glava, the Transylvanian, is buried in one of those graves and is held responsible for the death of "Billie," who had visited Glava's grave every Halloween for ten years. The long-haired vampire Glava tries to kill Billie's friend Janice by visiting her dreams. Janice's friend Richard confronts Glava, who is wielding a pointed wood stake, but Glava escapes. Undaunted, Richard buys an antique revolver filled with silver bullets and confronts Glava, once again prepared to cause havoc with his wood stake. To defeat the demon, Richard fires the fatal shot into Glava's heart.

"Vampire Hunting in Colorado"
by Nerdy Sarah
nerdysarah23.blogspot.com
May 15, 2013

The legend: Todor Glava, a vampire, came to Colorado to work in the coal mines "and sent money back to his wife in Austria." Because of his lack of money, his tombstone is shared with another man from Romania. Local legends say Todor rises from the grave "to this day" and can be seen sitting on the gravestone.

"This legend does not mix with any of the others because a dead vampire does not rise or randomly appear; this isn't a ghost we're talking about. There is a tree that grows right out of the ground where the chest of Todor Glava is; this is rumored to be from the stake that was driven through his heart and killed him. Like I said: a dead vampire does not rise.

"The legends also do not include any part of how he might have become a vampire. I'm pretty sure a vampire in a coal mine would be an obvious thing, that's a lot of people in a little space. But that does give him a dark space to live and an excuse to never go out."

"There's a Vampire Buried in Lafayette?," 9news.com
January 16, 2015

The legend: At the time of Transylvanian immigrant Fodor Glava's death in 1918, "stories started swirling. Some folks assumed Glava was a vampire.

"A tree, supposedly, mysteriously grew up from the grave where his heart would have been, and people wondered if there wasn't a stake driven through his heart because they thought he was a vampire."

"The Transylvanian Vampire Mystery in Colorado Still Baffles People Today," OnlyInYourState.com
May 17, 2017

The legend: According to several Coloradans, there may be a vampire in the Lafayette Cemetery.

"Mr. Glava's grave is plagued with mystery, as legend has it that the former coal miner, who was tall, pale and had abnormally long fingernails, was in fact a real vampire. While his 'vampire-like' appearance can be written off as merely being an ill man during a trying time in American history, the fact that a large tree grew from the center of his grave is the cherry on top of this Boulder County mystery."


"THE LAFAYETTE VAMPIRE," ROCKYMOUNTAINPARANORMAL.COM
JANUARY 30, 2018

The legend: The grave is said to contain the vampires "Glavia and Trandafir," who were originally from Transylvania. There are reports of batteries draining when near the grave, a shadow figure standing at the grave, a tree growing from the stake in the vampire's heart, disembodied voices and strange lights and roses growing at the site from the vampires' fingernails.

The "research": The stories of the vampire appeared in the 1960s after a headstone had been placed on the plot to appear as though a tree was growing from the center of the grave. "Batteries remain okay when we're near the site, and there are no EMF variances.

"Current stories only coming from ghost hunters who are looking for the vampire and not the locals who are in the area all the time. This explains how this urban legend is still spreading even though the locals have realized that this is not a claim based in reality."


"PSSST. GET SCARED AT THESE SEVEN REAL HAUNTED PLACES IN
    COLORADO," THEDENVEREAR.COM
OCTOBER 6, 2018

The legend: In Lafayette, there's an old cemetery purchased for paupers, including Fodor Glava. "Local lore" says that he was a vampire and a stake was driven in his heart to "keep him from rising and causing havoc."

"Local kids report seeing a tall dark figure sitting atop the grave. Paranormal investigators have caught pictures of orbs floating around the headstones and voices hissing from another world. You might visit the grave, but perhaps you should be sure to eat something with a little garlic beforehand—just to be on the safe side."

"Five Most Haunted Places in Colorado," OurCommunityNow.com
October 28, 2019

The legend: Lafayette, Colorado, has a vampire buried in the cemetery, and "the local legend is more than just hearsay, as there's an actual grave to go with the tale." Not much is known about Fodor Glava other than that he was a miner in town seeking work and became a victim of the Spanish flu outbreak. "He died in Lafayette and is one of a very small number to have a headstone. Local lore tells the tale of a dark figure who sits atop the grave on dark nights, and those who grew up in the area are quite familiar with the story."

"Vampire Grave in Lafayette, Colorado Cemetery,"
    ATravelForTaste.com
by Karren Doll Tolliver
January 21, 2020

The legend: A tree grows from the stake in the heart of Fodor Glava, a vampire.

"Some people claim to have seen the vampire himself, and a few paranormal investigative teams have looked into it with inconclusive results, but have reported wildly fluctuating readings on their equipment."

The research: "Of course I don't believe that Fodor Glava was actually a vampire." The name etched in the upper left of the stone, Trandatir, "is a Romanian word that means 'rose.' So it's possible that Fodor's wife's name was Trandatir (Rose) and that she died about the same time as he did and was (supposed to be) buried next to him. It could also explain why there were rose bushes growing around the headstone."

"The Famous Vampire Grave at Lafayette Cemetery," Kindred
    Spirit Society International
www.kindredspiritsociety.org
June 2020

The legend: A vampire grave belongs to "Mr. Fodor Glava," who died "in 1908." The legend is that a stake was driven into his heart and out of it grew a tree.

"Vampire Grave of Lafayette," AtlasObscura.com
by Devin San Luis
June 4, 2020

The legend: Theodore "Fodor" Glava was a tall, pale and lanky Transylvanian immigrant. After he died in 1918, local lore says that some townspeople dug up his grave and found blood by Glava's mouth and that his teeth were larger than normal. Settlers drove a stake through his heart and reburied him. Now a tree, unlike any other around it, grows from the grave plot. Some say it grew from the wood stake.

"Rumors even persist to this day that residents from the local area see a mysterious figure walking around late at night. So who is to say if he was a vampire or nothing more than an innocent man caught up in wild superstition. If you do go looking for yourself, bring Fodor a small gift, a coin, a trinket or maybe even a bouquet of dead roses…just leave the garlic at home."

"Grave of a Vampire," Virily.com
by Sandra Rasma
2020

The legend: A particular grave appears to contain a vampire. A tree grew out of the stake "that once killed the vampire" and "people have seen a tall, slender man with dark hair dressed in a dark coat who has long fingernails and is seen sitting on the tombstone." A coal miner named Fodor Glava purchased the plot and died in 1918. "It turns out he might not have been buried there.

"Even though you might not believe so, you go to this cemetery defiant to prove it is all a hoax and then what do you do when you do come face to face with this vampire? There is always that to consider too."

"There's a Real Vampire Grave in Colorado and It Will Make Your Blood Run Cold if You See It," ImFromDenver.com
August 5, 2021

The legend. Teodor "Fodor" Glava died on May 12, 1918. No one knows how he died, but he's buried under a headstone that reads "Mr. Fodor

Glava" located north of the Lafayette Cemetery. The headstone is polished black marble with an intricately carved border around it. He bought the plot himself in July 1911.

"Locals say you can find him at night when he leaves his grave—that red roses grow around where his heart would've once rested during life too, though nobody knows why. People living in Lafayette have long been creeped out by the grave, and kids—or adults—like to dare each other to stand near it."

"Legend Says a Vampire Is Buried in This Colorado Cemetery," TownSquareNoCo.com
by Kelsey Nistel
September 16, 2021

The legend: A vampire by the name of Fodor Glava is buried in the Lafayette Cemetery. Glava, while living, was described as tall, pale man with noticeably long fingernails. A tree now grows from the center of his grave. Visitors have seen a tall, thin man walking around the cemetery.

"Theodor 'Fodor' Glava: The Lafayette Vampire," RandomTimes.com
September 27, 2021

The legend: An inscription "born in Transylvania" etched in stone "would invite vampire comparisons, but the people of Lafayette have really gone all out." There's a tall, thin man sighted on the gravestone, rosebushes said to have been from his fingernails, and a tree growing where a stake was placed in his heart. Locals found blood on Fodor's mouth when they dug him up, after which they put a stake through his heart and reburied him. "Rumors even persist to this day."

The "research": Fodor, when he was alive, was a pale, lanky Transylvanian immigrant. He along with another man is buried on the north edge of the cemetery, a burial that "caused the whole town to be quarantined." Transylvania, where Fodor is from, is associated with Vlad the Impaler, Count Dracula and vampires galore.

"THE CREEPY, OBSCURE HISTORY OF 'THE COLORADO VAMPIRE,'"
 *GAZETTE* (COLORADO SPRINGS, CO)
BY TAMARA TWITTY
WWW.GAZETTE.COM
OCTOBER 25, 2021

The legend: Todor Glava is buried in the Lafayette Cemetery, and "rumors persist" that he may have been a vampire. His hand-carved headstone has a "single, spindly tree" growing behind it. "Location stories" suggest townspeople dug up his body and found that "his teeth were abnormally long, he had blood on and in his mouth, and his fingernails never stopped growing." As a result, townspeople drove a stake in his heart, out of which "a tree growing near his plot…sprouted from the stake." Further, "there is no recorded evidence to substantiate this story."

"Along with the story comes a history of supernatural sightings at Todor's gravesite. A tall, dark figure believed to be the spirit of Todor Glava has been reported lingering around stone on occasion ever since." (The online story links to another article from the same author stating that "children have seen a tall, dark figure lingering around the stone.")

"LAFAYETTE'S VAMPIRE, A 1918 SPANISH FLU VICTIM," *COLORADO CONNIE*
 (BLOG)
BY COLORADO CONNIE
WWW.COLORADOSTORIES.ONLINE
OCTOBER 26, 2021

The legend: Rumors persist that Lafayette residents see a mysterious figure walking around the cemetery at night. "Lore tells us" that locals dug up his grave, found blood on his mouth and his nails still growing, and they placed a stake through his heart. Out of the stake grows a tree, although "there are trees all around although none grow straight through his plot."

The "research": Local families would have picnicked in the cemetery on Sundays. And, hark, there is a good and factual explanation (yes, finally!) of the fictional history of vampires starting with the poem "The Bride of Corinth in 1797."

"The Myth of the Lafayette Vampire," YellowScene.com
by Zoe Jennings
October 7, 2021

The legend: A tree grows from the center of a grave of an immigrant coal miner from Transylvania. Locals allegedly dug him up and ran a stake through his heart. Out of it sprouted a "jupiter tree."

The research quoted in the story: According to Lafayette Miners Museum director Krista Barry, "The likelihood that Todor Glava was believed to be a vampire in 1918 when he died was pretty slim to begin with. The fact that he dies in 1918 during a pandemic, and it says in his obituary that he was sick and he died of the flu, I don't think too many people were worried about staking him back in the day."

"Old Town Haunted History Tour," What's Her Name (podcast)
by Olivia Meikle
whatshernamepodcast.com
October 2020

The online phenomenon of audio podcasting is last in line for the re-re-retelling of the Lafayette vampire tale. The Old Town Lafayette Haunted History Tour, co-sponsored by the Lafayette Historical Society, is an annual walking tour along East Simpson Street offered in the days and weeks leading up to Halloween. An October 2020 recorded and self-guided version of the tour resides online.

Produced in the midst of heavy-duty societal anxiety surrounding the COVID-19 pandemic—and its "invisible assailant"—the Old Town audio walking tour podcast includes the Lafayette Vampire, but its local legend "enhancements" of a vampire running rampant top all others and illustrate how legends are modified to reflect the time period.

"The [vampire] legend gets its upstart in 1960s—then just pops up out of nowhere. At the turn of the century, a Transylvanian vampire was running amok in Lafayette, mass death, chaos, terror…and the local community banded together and staked him in the heart, and buried him in Potter's Field. As a result, a cedar tree grows from the stake out of his heart, and from his long fingernails grew blood-red roses. But don't get too close, there are reports of people being beaten up by an invisible assailant near the grave."

The podcast does go into some fact-based history to explain the Lafayette Vampire legend, which is the Great New England Vampire Panic rooted in eastern European folklore. Starting in the early 1800s, rural residents of New England disinterred corpses suspected of being victims of vampires. These disinterments correspond to severe tuberculosis outbreaks but sometimes happened years after someone died. The "de-vampirization" process involved cutting the head off the corpse and removing whatever was left of the heart and burning it, a process prescribed in folklore. Accounts of public square (town green) burnings of "vampire hearts" have been found. This kept the dead person from rising up and stalking other victims. Keep in mind that no one saw a vampire drinking blood or interacting with a live person; the sucking of blood from the victim always involved a mysterious, invisible agent. In modern medical terms, the vampire victims had in fact died of tuberculosis—known as consumption or wasting disease, because the victim literally wastes away, becoming thin, pale and fragile in the journey to death. And blood around the lips and teeth is always a symptom, as the dying person coughs up blood.

So the East Simpson Street audio tour's explanation of mobs chasing down an active vampire don't square with either the "old school" Lafayette legend or the Great New England Vampire Panic, which involved buried corpses being dug up. And we know that Teodor Glava didn't die from tuberculosis, but rather Spanish flu. (The affliction was still mysterious but didn't involve a wasting disease.) And, ironically and unfortunately, the historical society's walking tour—in person and self-guided—spells doom for some of Simpson Street's old buildings, because it resurrects the long-standing stereotype that a derelict building with "serious negative energy" is evil and therefore haunted. It wouldn't be a haunted tour otherwise.

## How We Got Here

The origins of the Lafayette Vampire, as with any other vampire tale ever told, goes back two millennia in the eastern European areas of what are now Romania, Estonia, Latvia and Lithuania. Transylvania sits in the upper region of Romania, embraced on all sides by the Carpathian Mountains.

The locus of centuries of war and overrun by Goths, Huns, Gepids, Slavs, Bulgars, Magyars (Hungarians), Cumans, Greeks, Romans and Mongols, the region defined as Transylvania was desirable because of its mineral wealth, including gold, copper and iron.

The region's folklore describes a formless demon that caused drought by sucking water from the clouds. This transitioned into a demon that sucked blood from humans and reanimated the corpses, an anthropomorphic variation to explain unexplained physical frailties. There was no such thing as modern medicine, so wasting diseases such as tuberculosis and celiac disease meant that something otherworldly was draining the victims' blood and killing them. The vampire itself, the sucking of blood and the reanimation were never witnessed, but rural villagers believed something demonic was afoot.

There's a clear boundary separating the ancient folkloric vampire and the cinematic and literary versions rooted in the early nineteenth century.

The first use of the word *vampire* in the Oxford English Dictionary comes in 1734, when these creatures were described as "evil spirits who animate the bodies of deceased persons." Several Gothic-era literary representations of the vampire tale, English-language precursors to Bram Stoker's classic book *Dracula*, debuted in the early to mid-1800s. These include John William Polidori's *The Vampyre* (1819, see Appendix A), Ames Malcom Rymer's *Varney the Vampire* (1845) and Sheridan Le Fanu's book about a female vampire, *Carmilla* (1872).

Bram Stoker's 1897 book *Dracula*, the template for almost every vampire book and movie made after it, reflected post–Victorian era medical anxieties and society's exhaustion with the Industrial Revolution, which promised great things but seemed to be falling short; tuberculosis, cholera and bubonic plague ran rampant in major cities.

Stoker based his book on the real-word journals penned in A.F. Crosse's *Round about the Carpathians*. Published in 1878, the anti-Semitic travelogue details culture and traditions of rural villagers inhabiting Romania's (or Austro-Hungary's) Transylvania region. Stoker, who was Irish and never visited Transylvania, relied on Crosse's detailed descriptions of the mountainous typography and of the dress and mannerisms of the locals.

Stoker's classic reflects the anti-Semitic and anti-immigrant dynamics of late-1800s England. Dracula comes from elsewhere, so he's the embodiment of epidemics. He brings swarms of rats and a terrifying, blood-thinning illness that corrupts the race and is the poster child of what wealthy elitists at the time termed the "swarm of races," specifically eastern European Jewish migrants who the elitists said were destroying the East End of London with their "physical and moral infections."

*Dracula*'s commonality with the handful of early published works is its establishment of "vampire rules." Rather, these are the rules to follow to avoid the beast and eliminate it. The common element is the precise, folklore-

Front cover of a 1919 edition of Bram Stoker's *Dracula*, showing Dracula the vampire crawling headfirst down the castle wall. *Wikimedia Commons, public domain.*

based method for destroying the vampire: a stake through the heart, the head removed and placed on the chest and the heart removed and burned by fire (see Appendix B). Stoker's Dracula, an undead vampire, is described as tall, thin and pale with prominent, sharp teeth and possessing a host of supernatural abilities. He casts no shadow and has no reflection in a mirror. He's immortal, can control weather and wildlife (wolves particularly), controls people telepathically who have fallen victim to his bite, controls people telepathically who haven't fallen victim to his bite, can transform into animals (especially bats) and into clouds and mist and has anti-gravity skill sets (being able to easily crawl headfirst down castle walls).

The notion of vampire lore gaining a foothold in early 1900s east Boulder County is not likely. Although *Dracula* sold for fifty cents at the Daniels & Fischer Stores Company in downtown Denver, it's unlikely the book was a popular read, or available, in Lafayette. There's no mention of anything having to do with *Dracula* in the local newspapers, and the book was not readily available—there was no bookstore, and the town's public library didn't open until 1923. (Even then, the local Methodist church's Reverend J.C.B. Hopkins procured and reviewed the library's books.)

Lafayette town founder Mary E. Miller did operate Woman's Christian Temperance Union reading rooms in Lafayette and Louisville from about 1890 until about 1910, but a book describing "the undead" would not have been on the reading rooms' shelves. Vampires were mentioned in the *Lafayette News* (founded 1898) only a handful of times from 1900 through 1920. Not until the vampire movies hit the Lafayette theater in the 1930s did residents get a full picture of the mythical bloodsuckers. Well, at least Hollywood's version.

It's possible that a copy of Bram Stoker's *Dracula* was passed around Lafayette, a town where everyone went to church, but not to the extent that a mob would organize in 1918 to dig up or even chase a Transylvanian. And if townspeople did suspect the local vampire fit the novel's description, one would think that the staking of a vampire would have followed the eastern European traditions Stoker describes—meaning, the head comes off!

Illustration from *Vikram & Vampire* by Ernest Henri Griset, 1870. *Wikimedia Commons, public domain.*

There is some historical fact associated with the fictional character of Dracula. Stoker got the name *Dracula* from Vlad the Impaler, or Vlad III Dracula, a fifteenth-century military governor of the historical Wallachia region of Romania. Vlad III is known in history for impaling his captured enemies on stakes buried in the ground. After one battle, he left thousands of impaled enemy soldiers as a deterrent to pursuing Ottomans.

Several decades after Stoker's *Dracula* was published, it made a noteworthy transition to cinema. The 1922 German silent movie *Nosferatu: A Symphony of Horror* was the embodiment of Germany's losing World War I. The life force was drained from the country, so no better time to debut a gangly vampire who drains the life force of people. Bram Stoker's widow, Florence Balcombe, successfully sued, claiming copyright infringement, and *Nosferatu* was removed from distribution and copies were destroyed. (Modern versions of the movie are an assemblage of bits and pieces of the film spared from destruction.)

Bela Lugosi's classic portrayal of Dracula debuted in 1931, during the Great Depression. Born in Romania, Lugosi isn't physically threatening, and his character doesn't reveal fangs but is nonetheless menacing, a product of his ability to hypnotize victims. Instead of the animated corpse portrayed in *Nosferatu*, Lugosi's Dracula is a debonair and handsome yet mysterious man with enchanting eyes. Even today, there's recognition of Lugosi kick-starting contemporary goth subculture.

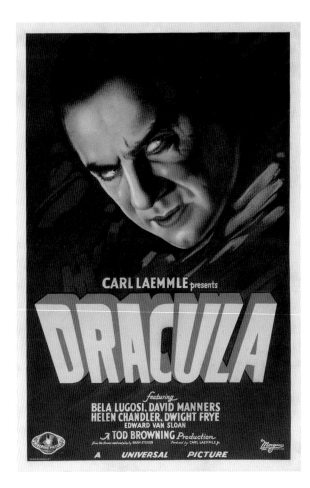

Movie poster for Carl Laemmle's *Dracula*, starring Bela Lugosi, 1931. *Wikimedia Commons, public domain.*

Just like the Bram Stoker version of the vampire in the wake of the Industrial Revolution, Bela Lugosi's 1931 portrayal found favor in an anxious populous devastated by a failed economy. The greedy, corrupt and selfish industrialists who caused the stock market crash were equated with the greedy, gluttonous vampire who preys on innocent victims.

The 1931 *Dracula* release was the first cinematic version of the vampire legend to hit Lafayette newsstands. The March 6, 1931 *Lafayette Leader* describes the Tabor Theater in Denver playing "'Dracula,' a sensationally different, weird and startling story of life after death, and the strange human vampires who rise from the graves at night and bring terror to the hours of darkness." At that time, it was easy to commute via railroad to and from Denver.

The first vampire movie advertised locally, by the LaFay Theater at East Simpson and Gough Avenue in Lafayette, was *The House of Frankenstein*, in

"Dracula" The Vampire Thriller Next At Tabor.

The next attraction at the Tabor Theatre, starting March 6th, according to previewers, is a picture which is absolutely in a class by itself,

It is "Dracula" a sensationally different. weird and startling story of life after death, and the strange human vampires who rise from their graves at night and bring terror to the hours of darkness.

Tabor Theater in Denver announcement of the movie *Dracula* from a 1931 edition of the *Lafayette Leader*. *Colorado Historic Newspapers.org.*

the December 21, 1945 edition of the *Lafayette Leader*. The movie's plot is an epic "monster mash" of mad scientist versus Frankenstein versus Dracula versus the Wolf Man. John Carradine played Dracula, Glenn Strange played Frankenstein and Lon Chaney Jr. was the Wolf Man.

Although the Dracula character in *The House of Frankenstein* fits the classic Bram Stoker typecast, Carradine's portrayal is just a subsidiary plot device, a mechanism for revenge. He still has a thirst for blood and primarily seduces young women, but this vampire—and all of the other movie monsters on the screen during World War II—were subdued and far less scary, due to the American public's exposure to the horrors of real war. Because of this, horror films from the 1940s and early 1950s are generally considered the weakest of the genre.

In 1958, a significant shift in the portrayal of Dracula took shape after the British production company Hammer Films released the movie *Dracula*, with Christopher Lee playing the blood-sucking protagonist. This and Lee's subsequent portrayals of the vampire forego the classic Bram Stoker script —a gangly, mysterious man of nobility who drinks blood to survive—and instead reveal a confident, mesmerizing, charming, charismatic historian with fangs and sex appeal. He's still a monster, which we know, but movie audiences, including Lafayette residents, took joy in adapting and morphing the monster to fit their whims. An example is how Christopher Lee's Dracula dies. In the Bram Stoker novel, he's staked in the heart with a knife and dissolves into dust. Stoker's vampires can endure death and move around in daylight but are weaker. In the 1931 and 1957 screen classics, Dracula dies after being exposed to sunlight, particularly in the latter movie, when the Abraham Van Helsing character rips open the window drapes and lets the sun melt the vampire.

In her 1995 book *Our Vampires, Ourselves*, Nina Auerbach, professor of English at the University of Pennsylvania, analyzes the evolution of the vampire, from the folkloric version in which the creature is a parasitic but unseen bloodsucker who never ventures beyond his birthplace to contemporary cinematic portrayals of a vampire who sucks blood, is a world traveler and just wants to fit in with humankind. This adaptability promoted more variations of the "rules" that vampires, and vampire hunters, must follow. And it meant that the fictional character shifted and bobbed according to cultural norms and the storyteller's preference.

The strict structure of eastern European vampire folklore, handed down via oral tradition for millennia, was no more.

"Every age embraces the vampire it needs," according to Auerbach. And each generation or social transition creates its own variables and variations of the classic villain—how to spot the vampire, how to destroy it and how to keep it away. But the emergence of an erotic Dracula, as portrayed by Christopher Lee, reflects the nation's entrance into the sexual revolution after the publication of Alfred Kinsey's sex studies in the early 1950s. For teenagers, the late 1950s and early 1960s was a tug-of-war between greater freedom—automobiles to get around town and to and from school, combined with loosening parental curfews and more time with friends— and the structured conformity of suburbia. More freedom meant more opportunities to challenge authority. Just like Dracula.

Locally, the result in the period from the 1960s to the 1980s was more drama added to the Lafayette Vampire tale; the vampire gets more nimble and stronger. No longer just a transplant from the land of folkloric vampires, Transylvanian Teodor Glava becomes the vampire portrayed in cinema, with concerned mobs dead set on dealing with him. Even though there are trees growing out of a half dozen grave sites in the Lafayette Cemetery, the juniper tree coming out of Glava's grave means something. As does the rosebush. It doesn't matter that it was a yellow rosebush—it's nothing other than a menacing "blood red." And, surely, no one could have constructed and labeled a concrete headstone out of respect. It had to have been fashioned by the demon himself. And never mind that, due to the overgrown rosebush, it wasn't physically possible for a ghost, a vampire or a real person to sit on Glava's gravestone and be seen. ("He was sitting right there, I swear. My friend's friend said so.")

# The Juniper Tree

The variety of tree growing from Glava's grave kinda, sorta fits vampire fiction. The preferred wood for staking a vampire is juniper, which is the type of tree growing out of Glava's plot. Although the tree was probably only seventy to eighty years old in 2022, it is at least the right type. And for those counting the years since the 1918 burial, that means the tree started growing in the late 1930s. The date it sprouted or its rate of growth is moot, because the fictional tree-growth narrative can easily be adjusted to say that the stake grew underground for several decades then popped through the surface and thrived.

And, as some of the storytellers have acknowledged, there are many other grave sites in the Lafayette Cemetery with trees popping out of the torso of the corpse.

But a variation of the Lafayette Vampire tale from locals who were students in the 1950s and '60s doesn't include the stake with a tree growing from underground. Instead, the stake used to destroy the vampire was placed in the ground on top of the grave (with another stick) in the form of a cross. This was to keep the vampire buried.

## THE YELLOW, ER, BLOOD-RED ROSEBUSH

Folklore sometimes gets twisted enough to create contradictions, which calls for clever solutions to those contradictions. The rose growing on the grave of Teodor Glava is one example.

In the progression of Lafayette Vampire "enhancements," the tale of a shrub with "blood-red roses" growing from the vampire's long fingernails (or hair) seems to have started in the 1970s. It became a regular part of the legend passed among schoolchildren in the 1980s and shows up in most of the early 2000s and later published accounts. The first published mention of a foreboding rosebush is in the 1993 *Rocky Mountain News*, where the rosebush "blooms blood red in the spring." Although the roses were actually yellow, the legend had an alternative narrative: they glowed blood red on only one night a year. Halloween would have been an obvious night for the color switchover, but rose petals surviving until October 31 would be the exception rather than the rule. The green foliage on a rosebush can survive a hard freeze, but the flowers can't. So maybe it was one night during the summer. The legend isn't specific.

The yellow rosebush—minus its foliage due to fall and winter timing—is visible in October 1993 and October 2001 photographs of the grave site but was generally so large that the Trandafir-Glava grave marker was completely covered. The bush was described by longtime resident Frank Archuleta, who actually laid eyes on the flowering bush in the daylight and in the summer. He said it "glowed an unnatural bright yellow, almost like it was on fire." Nannette Iatesta, another longtime resident, also said that the rosebush was a yellow rose but of a wild variety. And the 1998 *Daily Camera* article about the vampire legend quotes the city parks director, who headed the department charged with maintaining the cemetery, as saying the roses were yellow.

Eyewitness accounts of the roses being yellow contrast with the legendary "locals say" or "this kid in school said" accounts, in which no one actually witnessed them being red. But the legend sounds better if they say that.

Yellow wild rosebushes are abundant in Lafayette. Known as "Harison's Yellow Rose," the variety thrives without pruning and grows up to eight feet tall and four feet wide. Locally, the Harison's rose is said to have been brought west from New York by coal miners settling in Lafayette. Hard-rock miners from the eastern United States also brought the plant to Colorado during the gold rush days of the 1860s. The Harison's wild rose is difficult to transplant, so someone likely transplanted and nurtured the Trandafir-Glava rosebush in its formative stages.

The rosebush was at the head of the grave plot, on the west side of the concrete grave marker. Judging from city cemetery records, the bush spanned five grave sites from north to south, with a rough dimension of eighteen feet long by six feet wide. A 1979 image of the grave site shows the rosebush centered about five feet to the north of Glava's marker, meaning that it was planted many feet north of his grave. No one knows for certain when the rosebush was removed, but no trace of it remains in 2023.

"Trandatir" scratched into the grave marker is an alternate spelling of "Trandafir," a Romanian term derived from the Greek language meaning "rose." Historical interpretation of the Lafayette Vampire legend has suggested that Trandafir was Teodor Glava's wife and was buried alongside him. We know this is not factual, because on his September 1918 military draft registration card, Teodor Glava lists "Sofich Glava" as his wife and her place of residence as the Hunedoara region of Hungary (the Transylvania region of Romania). Probate records at the Colorado State Archives detailing settlement of Glava's estate also show that "Sophia Glaver" was Teodor's wife. His daughter is listed as "Victoria (Glaver) Codrean." Both lived in Romania when Teodor died in 1918.

It's possible that a friend or relative of John Trandafir planted a rosebush as a memorial. Alternatively, superstition may have played a role, in that a rose was planted to prevent the alleged vampire from rising from the grave. But the Lafayette vampire folklore that the wild rosebush grew from the vampire's fingernails or hair conflicts with anti-vampire instructions described by the fictional characters in Bram Stoker's *Dracula*. In chapter 3, Jonathan Harker describes being given a wild rose and garlic by villagers as anti-vampire charms as he traveled to Dracula's castle. In chapter 18, Dr. Van Helsing states that a wild rose needs to be placed over the corpse to keep the vampire from rising from the dead.

So vampires pretty much hate roses, including the smell, the thorns and the lack of mobility thing—truly everything about them. So why would a rosebush spontaneously sprout from the vampire himself? ("But Doug, you missed the part of the Lafayette Vampire legend where the rosebush sprouted not from the fingernails but from the rose branch buried above Glava.")

## THE FIGURE IN THE BLACK COAT

What about the ghostly, thin figure, supposedly the vampire, sitting on the grave marker or walking near the grave?

Among the scant documents concerning Teodor Glava is his September 18, 1918 draft registration card, filled out about two months before his death. All men age eighteen to forty-five were required to register in person for the World War I draft, whether or not they were naturalized citizens. Lafayette had 341 draftees register, and the September 13, 1918 *Lafayette Leader* stated that "every man seemed anxious to get his name on the roll and most of them expressed the hope that the government would need their service and call them at once."

Glava's responses on his draft card describe him as medium height (the other options being tall or short) and medium build (not slender or stout). Medium height in the early 1900s was in the range of five feet, six inches to six feet. A man over six feet was considered tall. And Glava certainly wasn't "slender" or "thin."

He's described on the draft card as a "non-declared alien," meaning that he did not intend to seek U.S. citizenship. He describes himself as a citizen of Hungary, born on August 1, 1877. He lists his nearest relative as "Sofich Glava," living in "Les, Hunedora, Hungary." The draft card is signed by Glava as "Teodor Glava," and the person who filled out the card wrote Teodor's name as "Theodore Glava."

Enhancements to the Lafayette Vampire tale include a description of the living, breathing Glava as being tall and thin and having long fingernails. It would not be possible to conduct the demanding, manual physical labor of shoveling and sorting chunks of coal with anything but trimmed nails. Additionally, as a general rule, coal miners (like Glava) were short, as the areas where coal was mined often had less than six feet in clearance. A short coal miner didn't have to bend over to do the work. A tall coal miner would have been miserable and would not have mined for more than a few weeks before begging to be transferred to aboveground tasks.

Glava was a coal miner for sure. In addition to his death notice stating that he worked at the Simpson coal mine, the May 17, 1918 *Lafayette Leader* has "Tudor Glavor" listed among several dozen Simpson workers who contributed $100 to the local Liberty bond drive. War bonds were sold to citizens throughout the country to raise money to finance the nation's involvement in World War I. A "John Trandafer" is listed as contributing $50.

A "lost soul" wandering the grave site, described by the nineteen-year-old expert vampirologist in the 1993 *Rocky Mountain News*, is contrary to the fictional creature described in the vampire guidebook, Bram Stoker's *Dracula*. In that book, vampires technically have no souls, so a vampire spirit wandering the cemetery wouldn't be a lost soul, but rather—I guess—a lost "it." (Maybe it's just me, but shouldn't a vampire expert know every detail of Stoker's *Dracula*?)

## EARLY IMMIGRANTS

Setting the stage for revealing the real-life, mortal men who were Teodor Glava and John Trandafir, one needs to understand the nation's—and Lafayette's—xenophobic attitudes of the early 1900s. That period saw a dramatic increase in European immigration. In 1907, a record 1.2 million Europeans arrived in the United States, with 1 million each year in 1913 and 1914. With this increase came cheap and almost unlimited labor, even in the far reaches of the Northern Coal Field in Lafayette, Louisville and Erie. With that came fear and resentment. Add to this the First World War and the U.S. entry into that war in 1917; everyone who'd immigrated from the former Austro-Hungarian Empire was viewed as an enemy (my ancestors included).

Starting with the coal strike of 1910, the Long Strike, the local coal companies wanted a way to procure cheap, non-union labor. Notices and recruiters were sent to the coal regions of Missouri, Pennsylvania and the Southeast, as well as the coal mining areas of eastern Europe, including Romania. The coal companies accommodated the travel, and the immigrant and migrant miners could work off the travel debt with their labor.

Animosity toward immigrant strikebreakers, or scabs, in the 1910s is described in a 1975 oral history from Welsh immigrant "Welchie" Mathias, a union coal miner who was on strike during the Long Strike.

"Whenever they [the scabs] come up [from the Simpson Mine to Old Town], they'd be getting their pay, and they'd head for the saloons up here," said Mathias. "Well, we'd try to roll them, you know, get whatever we could from the bastards. Out [of a saloon] this sonofabitch comes, you know, with six bottles of beer, under each arm wrapped up with a *Denver Post*, and just as he got to the corner [of Michigan and East Simpson] about six of us nailed that bastard. But he had me, see, he had me by the hair, but I was biting him on the leg. We got $70 out of that sonofabitch and went to Denver for 4th of July. Oh dear, it's more money than we ever knew existed."

The town board's management of indigents, or paupers, is revealed in town budgets and line-item expenditures from 1900 to about 1940. There's no explanation how the money was used or who the truly needy were, but line-item expenditures under the category of "pauper" were granted to merchants in town, probably to defray costs of merchandise provided to someone who couldn't afford it. In general, the expenditures reimbursed were in the range of two to five dollars and totaled in the hundreds of dollars per year, so the commitment was not large, but it wasn't small, either. And town founder Mary E. Miller is recognized for delivering food and goods to recent immigrants residing along Gooseberry Gulch, which was low-lying ground along East Emma and East Cleveland.

Shortly after the Long Strike and the union miners' unrest had subsided, the Spanish flu pandemic struck. Peaking in Lafayette at the end of 1918, the deadly virus intensified hatred and animosity directed at immigrants. In the media, an unidentified health department official in Denver placed partial blame for the pandemic on immigrants: "The foreign element gives us much trouble when an epidemic occurs. They pay no attention to the rules or orders issued by the health board in its effort to check the disease."

*Right*: A 1960 aerial image of the Lafayette Cemetery, showing the pre-1920 location of Potter's Field and Teodor Glava's grave site. *Author's collection; illustration by the author.*

*Middle*: Circa 1920s map of the Potter's Field; most of the graves in the list are illegible. *City of Lafayette cemetery archives.*

*Bottom*: Circa 1930s map of Potter's Field in the Lafayette Cemetery. It is a listing of burials with no locations given, hence the confusion about the exact location of Teodor Glava's burial. Note Glava's name listed at the bottom of the second column from the right. *City of Lafayette cemetery archives.*

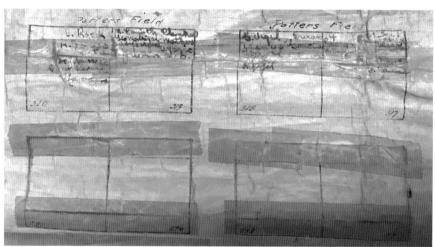

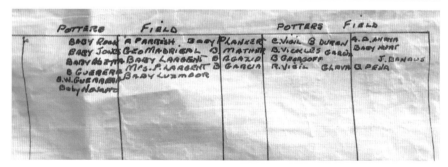

The local demonization of immigrant laborers started in the January 24, 1911 *Daily Camera*, when coal camps housing immigrant strikebreakers were described as places where "small pox and other epidemics are said to be raging in all their fury within the bull pens [the company housing] surrounding the mines."

And fear of some stranger from some other country—xenophobia—is evident in the Town of Lafayette's handling of burials at the Lafayette Cemetery.

When the Lafayette Cemetery was laid out about 1893, instructions were given to designate a Potter's Field area in the center portion of the north edge of the cemetery. It wasn't outside of the cemetery's boundaries, just at the north edge and, at the time, encompassed four cemetery blocks—317, 318, 319 and 320—about eight graves for each block or sixty-four grave sites total.

Early cemetery maps show that there are a couple dozen burials of "indigents," mostly stillborn or very young children from Latino families, in those cemetery blocks prior to Glava's 1918 burial. Personal accounts and 1950s photographic evidence shows that not many grave markers survived in the Potter's Field area. This means that the graves were either unmarked or that rudimentary wood markers had withered away and disappeared. Bev Smith recounted in a 2022 interview that as a child she visited her grandmother's Potter's Field grave, which was marked with a wood headstone, but the headstone weathered to dust a long time ago. In 2023, the grave can't be found.

Disturbingly, the scant city cemetery maps available do show a propensity by the Town of Lafayette to bury non-Protestant and nonwhite residents in Potter's Field rather than in the white, Protestant areas higher up on the hill (to the south). It didn't matter whether the deceased had money; we know from the estate records of Teodor Glava and John Trandafir that both had thousands of 1918 dollars in savings. If they were Catholic, Eastern Orthodox and eastern European, Mexican or native-born Latinos who'd moved here from New Mexico, they were segregated and buried in Potter's Field.

## TEODOR GLAVA, THE ROMANIAN

We have a couple clues as to Teodor Glava's birthplace. One is the primitive grave marker that states that "Todor Glava" was born in Transylvania.

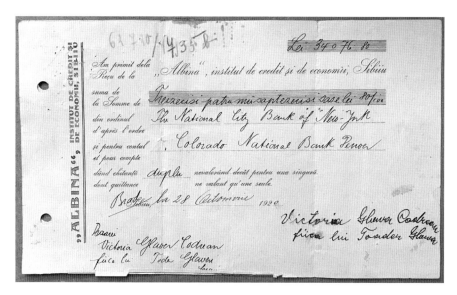

The 1920 bank receipt of the wire transfer of proceeds of Teodor Glava's estate sent to his daughter, Victoria, living in Hunedoara, Romania. His wife, Sophia, also resided in Romania, and she received proceeds of the estate totaling $835.40. *Boulder District Court archives at the Colorado State Archives, Denver.*

Immigration documents associated with Glava's relatives also help us track his whereabouts after his arrival in the United States, but those documents are sparse.

Like hundreds of eastern European immigrant coal miners working in east Boulder County mines, Teodor Glava had no family in the United States. His 1918 draft card, on which he signed his name as "Teodor Glava," lists his nearest living relative as "Sofich Glava," living in "Les, Hunedoara, Hungary." His death notice mentions that his wife was in Austria, which was used interchangeably with Hungary and Romania when all of those countries were in the Austro-Hungarian Empire.

According to Romanian genealogist Dan Jurca, Hunedoara County is in the Transylvanian region of today's central Romania and borders the Carpathians. "Les" is probably either Lesnic or Lelese. Alternate Romanian names for Lelese are Leles, Lelesz and Seles.

"Lesnic is found on the Mures valley, far away from any mining industry," said Jurca in a 2022 interview. "But Lelese is found in an area (Tinutul Padurenilor) close to the iron mines of Teliuc and Hunedoara. These are mines and industry with a long history in the area that goes back at least two thousand years. The area of Lelese is also famous for the quarry mines (white marble). From Lelese area to Valea Jiului [the coal mining region] is at least sixty kilometers (about thirty-seven miles). So Teodor could have worked as a miner in his own region of Lelese, but it's highly improbable he commuted to Valea Jiului for coal mining."

We don't know if Teodor Glava had experience with mining before he arrived in the United States, but if his Romanian residence was Lelese, then he could have been an experienced miner and a desirable recruit in the coal mines of West Virginia and Colorado. And it's likely he would have seen or heard of the U.S. recruiters willing to pay transportation costs from Europe to the land of opportunity.

A "Toader Glava" is listed on the Ellis Island arrival manifest for the *Kronprinz Wilhelm*, which left for the United States from Bremen, Germany, in 1914. He's listed as the cousin of passenger Petru Dinis, who lists a hometown in Fulesd, Hungary, now associated with northeast Romania (but not Transylvania).

Another male on the same voyage, Rosalim Gros, also lists "Toader Glava" as a cousin. Gros lists his hometown as Stoieneasa, a town in Hunedoara County in the Transylvania region of Romania. The *Kronprinz Wilhelm* arrival manifest at Ellis Island lists Gros's final destination as "Gary, West Virginia, where his cousin Toader Glava resides."

Gary, West Virginia, is a mining town located in the midst of fourteen mines that supplied coal to industrial giant U.S. Steel. In 1907, coal companies hired a recruiter to bring workers from Europe, including Italians, Hungarians, Poles, Austrians and Russians. Coal companies operating in northern Colorado employed a similar strategy during the 1910 to 1914 Long Strike.

Glava eventually makes his way to the coal camp known as Canfield, Colorado, which is about one mile west of Erie and about two miles north of Lafayette. Glava's 1919 estate settlement records show that he rented a room in Canfield for $1.12 per day from coal miner Nick Mack and his wife, Elizabeth, who emigrated from Austria-Hungary (Romania) in 1913. The 1920 U.S. Census indicates that the Macks lived within a few houses of the Wise homestead and farm. Glava's best friend, John Long, a foreman at the Simpson Mine, where Glava worked, was the executor of Glava's estate.

Close-up of the right half of the Trandafir/Glava shared headstone. *Photo by the author, 2023.*

# TEODOR GLAVA'S ESTATE RECORDS

He was married, was of medium height and medium build and had brown eyes and black hair.

He died on December 3, 1918, not December 4, 1918, as the *Lafayette Leader* reported, and was buried on December 6.

He worked at the Simpson coal mine.

He wasn't a resident of Lafayette but, rather, lived in Canfield, a former mining camp west of Erie, and rented a room for $1.12 per day from Mr. and Mrs. Nick Mack.

His estate was valued at $2,000 in 1918 (about $40,000 in 2023 dollars). It was composed primarily of savings certificates, but he had $400 in war bonds.

He was embalmed then buried in the Lafayette Cemetery.

He was not destitute and not in need of government relief or public charity; there was no economic reason to bury him in "Potter's Field."

His best friend and the executor of the estate was John Long, a longtime supervisor at the mine.

Including the modest $100.00 casket, his funeral cost $181.44 (about $2,000.00 in 2023). The funeral included a minister and singers, which cost $8.00.

His personal effects at the time of death are described as not significant enough to inventory.

He was sick for two weeks before he died and was cared for by Dr. William J. Rothwell, the company doctor for the Simpson Mine.

There is no evidence that Glava bought a grave plot at the cemetery prior to his death, as it does not show up in the estate's asset inventory. His executor probably purchased the grave site for his burial, although there's no record of the transaction.

His wife is listed as Sophia Glaver; his daughter as Victoria Glaver Codrean. Both are listed as residing in Romania, and estate settlement funds were sent to a Romanian bank.

Close-up of the left half of the Trandafir/Glava shared headstone. *Photo by the author, 2023.*

# JOHN TRANDAFIR'S ESTATE RECORDS

He was single, was short in height and stout of build and had brown eyes and black hair.

He died on December 4, 1918, and was buried on December 8.

He worked at the Simpson coal mine.

He had lived in Lafayette "about four years."

His estate was valued at $1,400 in 1918 (about $27,500 in 2023). He had $800 in savings certificates and $250 in war bonds.

He was not destitute and did not need government relief or public charity; there was no economic reason to bury him in "Potter's Field."

His "next friend" and the executor of the estate was William J. Simpson of the Simpson Mine family, who was also chief of the Lafayette Fire Department. Simpson withdrew from the bank all the funds of the estate—$1,400 worth—and disappeared. Fortunately, William J. Simpson's bonding agents covered the theft, and John Trandafir's mother received the money due her from the estate.

He was embalmed and then buried in Lafayette Cemetery.

Including the modest $150 casket, his funeral cost $420 (about $8,200 in 2023). The funeral included a priest from the Greek Orthodox Church in Denver and a twenty-piece band.

His personal effects at the time of death included clothing valued at twenty-one dollars, a bed and pillows, a cornet and a Victrola record player valued at twenty dollars.

He was sick for ten days before he died and was initially cared for (probably at home) by Dr. William J. Rothwell, the company doctor for the Simpson Mine. He was then moved to a hospital in Denver, where he died.

Trandafir's best friend, Nick Gregoria, paid two dollars for Trandafir's grave plot in the Lafayette Cemetery.

His mother is listed as Elisabeta Trandafir living in Părhăuți, Romania. He had four brothers according to estate paperwork, not three, as the *Lafayette Leader* death notice stated, and "no relatives in this country."

## Adjustment Day Notice

Estate of Toder Glaver, deceased.

All persons having claims against said estate are hereby notified to present them for adjustment to the County Court of Boulder County, Colorado, on the 13th day of January, A. D. 1919.
12-13-4t                    JOHN LONG
Administrator of said estate.

## Adjustment Day Notice

Estate of John Trandafir, Deceased.

All persons having claims against said estate are hereby notified to present them for adjustment to the County Court of Boulder County, Colorado, on the 13th day of January, A. D. 1919.
WM. J. SIMPSON,
12-13-4t.    Administrator of said estate.

Notices of adjustments for the Glava and Trandafir estates. Both men died intestate, which meant their worldly possessions were subject to probate. Lafayette Leader, *December 1918.*

A November 1918 receipt of purchases on credit made by Teodor Glava at the Rocky Mountain Stores Company on East Simpson Street in Lafayette. The "bottles of Wurtzburger" are probably a near beer sold during the first few years of Prohibition. The remaining purchases are cigars, candy and nuts. *Boulder District Court archives at the Colorado State Archives, Denver.*

# Trandafir/Glava Cemetery Records

Teodor Glava's poured concrete grave marker is in the north-central one-fourth of the Lafayette Cemetery, the Potter's Field area, about midway between the eastern and western boundaries of the cemetery. But it might not be in the right spot.

Official cemetery records kept by the Town of Lafayette between 1900 and 1935 detailing burials of destitute and Latino residents are—in contemporary terms—a train wreck. If a family paid for a burial plot in the non–Potter's Field portion of the cemetery, a lot and space number were assigned, the deed recorded at the county clerk's office and a written receipt issued. If someone destitute or down on their luck couldn't afford a grave site or was labeled a "pauper," the town was casual and unconcerned about tracking the specific burial location in Potter's Field. A grave was dug, a burial took place, dirt went back on top and a name got recorded on a list. No lot number and no space number were recorded. Someone else could worry about the pesky details.

From official cemetery records we know that (1) Teodor Glava is listed as being buried in the Potter's Field section but without an exact location, and (2) there are no cemetery records whatsoever indicating where his fellow Romanian, John Trandafir, is buried. John Trandafir's estate documentation shows that a friend, Nick Gregorio, bought the two-dollar grave plot for Trandafir.

Glava shares the primitive concrete headstone marking Trandafir's grave, so he and Glava are most likely buried under or near the primitive headstone. But if anyone is relying on cemetery records for exactness, then it's possible Glava could be anywhere in Potter's Field. (The only way to positively identify who is under the headstone is to dig up the remains and compare the DNA with living relatives.)

The *Lafayette Leader* reported that "Theodore Glava" died on December 4, 1918, but Glava's estate records show that he died on December 3. The newspaper death notices reported that Teodor Glava died of influenza and John Trandafir died of pneumonia, both deaths likely the result of the 1918 flu pandemic. Estate records show that Glava had been ill for two weeks before he died, but the newspaper reported Glava "being better after being seen up town"—meaning that he probably visited Simpson Street merchants uphill from his workplace, the Simpson Mine. Trandafir was sick enough to be transported, probably by friends, to St. Joseph Hospital at Eighteenth and Humboldt in Denver, where he later died.

There's no explanation why Trandafir wasn't treated at the makeshift hospital set up in the Congregational church in Lafayette, which treated ninety people during the pandemic. Invoices for medical care in estate records indicate that both men were under the care of Simpson Mine company doctor William J. Rothwell, an experienced medical professional, which meant that the quality of care was second only to being at an actual hospital. Rothwell's close colleague and fellow company doctor, V.W. Porter, was recognized by the community as a hero for keeping Lafayette's flu deaths to a minimum. Porter would have treated patients regardless of faith, race or national origin. He's one of a handful of Lafayette residents who stood up against the Ku Klux Klan when that group wrested control of the Lafayette town board in the 1920s.

According to the Centers for Disease Control, an estimated 675,000 people died from Spanish flu in the United States; more than 50,000,000 died worldwide. Newspaper reports show that the number of local flu deaths was in the several dozens—not in the hundreds or thousands—and would not have necessitated mass burials, given that the Lafayette Cemetery had close to 4,500 available grave spaces (out of the roughly 5,000 buried in the cemetery as of 2022). All said, doctors employed by the Rocky Mountain Fuel Company provided Lafayette residents with exceptional health care during the 1918 pandemic, one of the reasons the community didn't suffer a greater number of deaths.

Lafayette Cemetery records show that in 1918 the going rate for an entire lot of eight grave spaces was $15.00, or about $1.88 per grave site ($36.80 per site in 2022). In other words, it was not expensive. (The average coal miner made $8.00 a day in 1918.) Cemetery records also show that in calendar year 1918, seven families and one entity, the United Mine Workers of America (UMWA), bought forty-four cemetery spaces total, about double the average yearly rate over the previous twenty years. (As of 2022, the UMWA burial spaces are unoccupied.) None of the spaces sold up to and including 1918 are recorded as being purchased by Trandafir or Glava.

# THE GRAVE MARKER

There's a primitive, poured-concrete memorial indicating Teodor Glava's possible burial location. Words scratched into the drying concrete—with misspellings—are "+ 2 Romanion, Trandatir, Born in Rarhouth, Bocvina" on the top left; "+ Todor Glava. Born in Translvania" on the upper right; and a shared "AustroHungaria. Died December 1918" on the bottom. The scratchings in the concrete indicate that the maker of the marker knew John Trandafir better than Teodor Glava. There's more detail about Trandafir, including his exact location of birth.

Determining the date of the grave marker is difficult. Generally, an average poured-concrete sidewalk on a city block can last from seventy to eighty years. But some sidewalks last only a few decades. The marker appears to be a combination of sand and Portland cement—indicative of mortar for masonry—because there are no signs of aggregate or gravel.

Because the newspaper death notices state that neither Glava nor Trandafir had relatives living in the United States, the Trandafir/Glava concrete marker was probably made by George Lazar, a friend. Lazar was a fellow immigrant from Bukovina, a region of Romania that's contiguous with but northeast of Transylvania. Lazar bought the grave site, bought flowers and candles for the graveside services and arranged for the music for the ceremony. He billed Trandafir's estate $37.50 for those items. Research indicates that in 1918, Lazar worked at a Rocky Mountain Fuel Company mine in Morley, Colorado. In 1942, Lazar filled out a draft registration

The 1942 military draft registration card filled out by John Tandafir's friend George Lazar, who organized Tandafir's graveside services in 1918. Note the similarity of lettering with the Trandafir/Glava gravesite marker on the following page. *Ancestry.com.*

Trandafir/Glava concrete grave marker in the Lafayette Cemetery. *Photo by Krista Barry, Lafayette History Museum.*

card and listed his address as Frederick, Colorado. Lazar's writing on the draft card—in block letters—matches the lettering on the Trandafir/Glava headstone. If Lazar did create the grave marker, he would have done it in the correct location, because he was in attendance at the graveside services.

| + 2 ROMANION | + TODOR GLAVA |
| :---: | :---: |
| TRANDATIR | BORN-IN |
| BORN-IN-RAR- | TRANSLVANIA |
| HAUTI-BOCVINA | |
| AUSTROHUNGARIA | |
| DIED DECEMBER | |
| 1918 | |

A modern-day enhancement of the grave's vampire angle, described in a 2009 visit to the grave site in the newsletter of the Kansas-based Bukovina Society of the America, stated that the block letters in the marker "were said to have been scratched into it by the long, sharp fingernail of the vampire." While there's no mention of how the vampire obtained and mixed the concrete, shoveled it in a wood frame and then hand-lettered the memorial, the Bukovina Society author does mention a "sapling" growing from the center of Glava's grave.

The "Rarhouti, Bocvina" description on the marker refers to Părhăuţi, Romania, which is in the Bukovina (also Bucovina) region of Romania. Trandafir's 1917 draft card lists his place of birth as "Pirvuct Justed Lucsava, Austria." (Trying to figure out the contemporary equivalent was futile, although "Justed" means "county.") Estate records show that John Trandafir's mom, Elisabeta Trandafir, and his four brothers, names unknown, lived in Părhăuţi, but the documents spell it "Perhaut," "Perhautz" and "Perhauti."

The marker's alignment with surrounding headstones suggests that the vertical line in the grave marker sits atop the dividing line of the grave spaces—Glava in the north four-by-nine-foot grave space and Trandafir in the south four-by-nine-foot space. Spanish flu deaths in 1918 had caused a shortage of caskets in parts of the United States, but not in Lafayette. According to local undertaker R.R. Powell's 1918 invoices, both Glava and Trandafir were buried in caskets, Glava first on December 6 and then Trandafir on December 8. Powell's invoices also show that Glava's casket was encased in "an outside box" and indicate that separate graves were dug for each and then filled in, Glava's first, then Trandafir's two days later. (Trandafir's funeral invoices also show the use of an "outside box" but don't say whether it was used for transporting him from Denver or for use in the burial.) Both men were in the height and weight range to fit an average casket (between twenty-four and twenty-eight inches wide). (They were both probably reasonably fit; they shoveled coal all day, after all.) This leaves a roughly two-foot margin between the caskets, which is where—in the margin—the grave marker is centered. Consequently, the juniper tree growing directly under Glava's side of the marker means it's growing in the margin—the empty space—between the two caskets and not out of Glava's heart or torso.

So the narrative of a stake in the heart is more like that of a stake in the thigh. But even that's a stretch.

The plus signs on the grave marker are Christian crosses used by the early Orthodox Greek Church. They're a derivative of pre-Christian Pythagoras crosses found in Greece. With arms of equal length, the Orthodox cross is not a symbol of the cross that Jesus died on but symbolized the four directions of spreading the gospel: north, south, east and west.

The "2" might signify that Trandafir or both men received the Orthodox Greek Church's second sacrament, or "chrismation," administered immediately after baptism. But the headstone could also mean that the grave marker applies to the two corpses buried in separate graves.

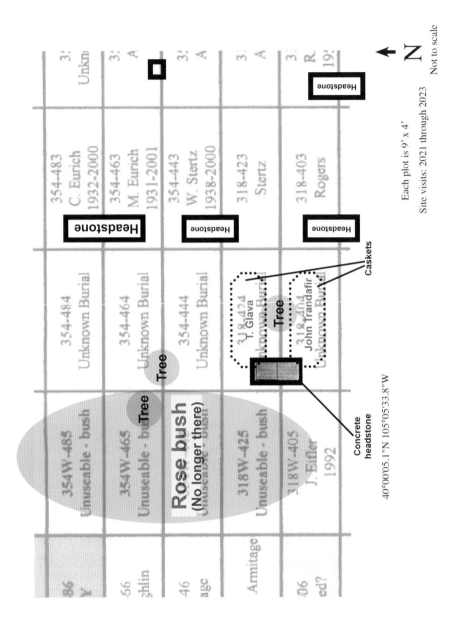

The Trandafir and Glava caskets and grave sites overlaid on a circa 2008 Lafayette Cemetery map. Note that the juniper tree is growing in the margin between the gravesites of the two men, not out of Glava's chest. *Illustration by the author, 2023.*

Receipts from their estates show that both men were embalmed and buried two days apart, Glava on December 6 and Trandafir on December 8. For Glava's graveside services, undertaker R.R. Powell charged ten dollars for "opening and filling grave." He invoiced a similar amount two days later for Trandafir's services for "opening and filling grave." Because of this, it's not likely that the two were buried side by side in one grave site. (A grave site is only four feet wide. Two caskets would not fit, even if the casket went in sideways and men lay shoulder to shoulder. They'd have to be propped up sideways in custom sixteen-inch-wide caskets.)

Burial receipts from the undertaker show that both men were buried in "plush caskets," which were wood caskets covered with fabric. Trandafir had a "plain cap lid casket," which is a casket in which just the top half of the lid opens. Both caskets were likely placed in their own wood "outside box," a sort of grave liner, then placed in their own individual grave plot. With two burials in adjacent plots two days apart, the undertaker's hired hand would have had a tough time digging the second grave. The dirt surrounding Glava's grave would have been unsettled and loose. A wood partition was probably built to keep the dirt from Glava's grave in place.

There are no available records from 1918 or 1919 indicating any special embalming or handling provisions in Colorado for someone who had died from the flu, and Lafayette did not set aside any particular area of the cemetery for burial of flu victims. (City records show they were dispersed throughout the cemetery.) There was a statewide quarantine in place that banned indoor assemblage but no ban on people gathering outside.

The complexity and prominence of Trandafir's services (a band was brought in from Denver), and a ceremony conducted under the auspices of the Orthodox Greek Church in Denver (following that church's strict liturgical parameters) means there's zero chance that church officials would have allowed Trandafir (buried in a casket on December 8) to be placed on top of the newly interred Glava (buried in a casket on December 6); something akin to a mass burial. This is especially true as there was no shortage of cemetery grave sites during the 1918 flu pandemic and no historical evidence showing that more than a few dozen people died and were buried in the cemetery in 1918. Additionally, the one entity in 1918 Colorado that could probably afford the $1.00 grave site fee for a pauper would be the Orthodox Greek Church.

Tellingly, though, estate records show that both Trandafir and Glava weren't paupers by any means and had thousands of dollars in savings. In 1918 terms, Glava had $2,028 in cash, war bonds and savings certificates; Trandafir had $1,400 worth of war bonds and savings certificates ($41,000 and $27,500 in

"The End of Life's Journey," by Boulder photographer Ed Tangen, circa 1909, showing the wood sign and entryway to the Lafayette Cemetery. *Courtesy Lafayette History Museum, Lafayette Historical Society.*

2023, respectively). This was more than enough to pay for a burial plot, casket and funeral. In fact, the total cost of Trandafir's funeral was $420 (about $8,200 in 2023). Even though Lafayette was still under quarantine, which forbade large indoor gatherings due to the influenza outbreak, Trandafir's graveside service was big. It included the twenty-plus-piece City Park Band from Denver (and prepaid tickets for their train fare), a hearse and modest casket, a canopy over the grave, muslin lining for the grave, car rental expenses for the pallbearers, an artificial flower wreath and the undertaker's fitting of Trandafir for burial with a new, black broadcloth suit.

So, Trandafir buried on top of Glava in a mass grave, or the men buried next to each other in one grave? No. Trandafir in a casket adjacent to Glava in a casket, and both in their respective grave sites? Yes.

## THE LAFAYETTE CEMETERY

Lafayette Cemetery records in the city's possession, maintained since the cemetery land was purchased from the Union Pacific Railroad in 1891, show burial plots at the north edge of the cemetery as "Potter's Field." By 1930, about two hundred spaces were being used for paupers' burials. The term

*Potter's Field* is of biblical origin and refers to an area where clay for pottery was collected but then became a burial ground for unclaimed, indigent or unknown persons.

The Potter's Field area first encompassed just two lots of the cemetery, 318 and 317, but expanded through the 1930s to include most of the northeast section of the cemetery. Grave plots in the north-central and northeast corners of the cemetery are poorly marked, on cemetery maps and in real life, with a mishmash of unknown graves. Of the five thousand persons buried at the Lafayette Cemetery, as many as 150 grave sites contain unknown persons.

In general, Lafayette Cemetery burials followed the Christian tradition of an east–west orientation, but headstones throughout the cemetery indicate that the head of the deceased was sometimes facing east and sometimes facing west.

City cemetery platting records show there are four lots per block and eight burial spaces (or grave sites) per lot, each being four feet tall and nine feet long (or wide). Cemetery rules allowed babies related to the deceased to be buried at the foot an adult grave. As of 2022, rules also allow a full-size adult to be buried along with an urn of ashes of a related party at the foot of the casket.

Typical burials for adults are six feet in depth. The small caskets for infants—and there are a lot of them in Potter's Field—were buried at shallower depths, usually two to three feet. Lafayette Cemetery did not require burial vaults for grave sites until the mid-1990s.

For grave sites in Potter's Field, there's evidence that up to four caskets of infants may have been buried side by side in one grave site. This means that there could be four unknown burials in one grave plot. And grave marking, especially for infants, has its limits. As is the case with cemeteries throughout time and around the world, a wood marker at the grave ages over time and decays to the point that it disappears. The same is true for stone markers, unless they're maintained or replaced.

There are no written cemetery records indicating that Glava or his family purchased a burial plot at the cemetery. An early map of the Potter's Field section, which probably dates to the mid-1930s, lists only twenty-three Potter's Field burials, composed of fifteen babies and eight adults. Glava is on the list, but we don't know if it's a guide to the actual burial location or just a list written in chronological order of death. John Trandafir isn't listed on any maps.

Above Glava on the cemetery map are burials—also lacking city documentation—of R. Vigil, Baby Georgoff, Baby Vickles, Garcia, C. Vigil and Baby Duran.

Teodor Glava's headstone sits on Block 318, Space 424, which is listed in 2023 city databases as an unknown burial but a space owned by the City

| O | P | Q | R | S |
|---|---|---|---|---|
| 359-546 Unuseable | 358W-545 Unuseable | 358-544 Unknown Burial | 358-543 Unuseable | 357-542 Unuseable |
| 359-526 Unuseable | 358W-525 Unuseable | 358-524 Unknown Burial | 358-523 Unuseable | 357-522 Unuseable |
| 355-506 CITY | 354W-505 Unuseable - bush | 345-504 Unknown Burial | 353-503 Unknown Burial | 353-502 Abrams |
| 355-486 CITY | 354W-485 Unuseable - bush | 354-484 Unknown Burial | 354-483 C. Eurich 1932-2000 | 353-482 Unknown Burial |
| 355-466 McLaughlin | 354W-465 Unuseable - bush | 354-464 Unknown Burial | 354-463 M. Eurich 1931-2001 | 353-462 A. Betz 1918 |
| 355-446 Armitage | 354W-445 Unuseable - bush | 354-444 Unknown Burial | 354-443 W. Stertz 1938-2000 | 353-442 Abrams |
| 319-426 Armitage | 318W-425 Unuseable - bush | 318-424 Unknown Burial | 318-423 Stertz | 317-422 Abrams |
| 319-406 occupied? | 318W-405 J. Eifler 1992 | 318-404 Unknown Burial | 318-403 Rogers | 317-402 R. Rosen 1955-2005 |
| 319-386 Rich | 318W-385 Eifler | 318-384 True | 318-383 Rogers | 318-382 Rogers |
| 319-366 Rich | 318W-365 J. Jung 1946-1999 | 318-364 True | 318-363 Rogers | 317-362 Rogers |
| 296-346 P. Rich 1926-1993 | 296E-345 CITY | 297-344 DeBruyne | 297-343 H. Rogers 1928-2003 | 298-342 L.W. Rogers 1954-2006 |
| 296-326 | 296E-325 | 297-324 | 297-323 | 298-322 |

Portion of City of Lafayette cemetery map showing modern location of Teodor Glava's gravesite, 318–424, labeled as "Unknown." *City of Lafayette cemetery archives.*

of Lafayette. There's also an unknown burial just below it (or south of it) at Block 151, Space 424, also owned by the city.

Interpreting the mid-1930s cemetery map listing geographically—as an actual location—Glava should be buried in Block 318, the fourth grave down from the top of the block on the east side, or the bottom righthand corner (plot 318–63 or 318–403). Modern cemetery records indicate that the burial plot 318–63 has the remains of Betty Rogers, who died in 2020. Her husband, Hugh R. Rogers, is in the burial plot south of her. Plot 318–403 is owned by the Rogers family.

# FINAL NOTE

If you, the reader, are disappointed with a slicing and dicing of this really shaky legend—pieces missing, no consistency, "experts" who are not experts—then so be it.

"But Doug," some say, "give it a rest. It's just for fun and amusement!"

I'm not in agreement. Teodor Glava was just a hardworking coal miner who wanted to make some money and return to his family in Romania. Instead, he was a victim of the 1918 flu pandemic.

In the summer of 2022, I placed an ad in the local newspaper asking former city employees who worked in the cemetery to provide snippets of their work experiences. Weird events? No weird events? It didn't matter. No former employees responded to the ad, but I did talk to several former city employees, including one whose mother lives near me. He didn't experience anything out of the ordinary.

The notice did garner a nice response from a Romanian immigrant who lives in Lafayette and voluntarily keeps Teodor Glava's grave site tidy. (The mementos and trash left at the grave the past few decades would fill a room.)

A cherub protects the grave site of a 2019 Lafayette Cemetery burial. Behind the cherub is Teodor Glava's grave site with the juniper tree. *Photo by the author, 2023.*

She felt that my perpetuating the Lafayette Vampire myth wouldn't do anything but sully the reputation of an ordinary man. I explained that I just wanted to dispel everything about the myth so that an ordinary man can be left alone. If the myth is not dispelled, and given the rate that the vampire fantasy has accelerated, there's a truly awful possibility of Teodor Glava's grave having to be fenced off to prevent adoring followers from destroying it.

## A Final, Final Note: The Author's Version of the Lafayette Vampire Legend, Which Is Just as Valid as Anyone Else's

The post-1970s enhancement of the Lafayette Vampire legend surmises that Glava wasn't a vampire when he died—his death notice reports that he died of natural causes, namely, pneumonia. Instead, residents feared he had been bitten by a vampire and would turn into one and rise from the grave. This means there was a "true" vampire stalking around Lafayette biting people and possibly creating a nest of vampires. (Who knows, they may still be around! Have you noticed that your neighbor doesn't age?)

Also, for argument, we can assume a full-fledged vampire would have been immune to the Spanish flu. Right? And the timing of the heart staking—after he's buried, not before—confirms that he wasn't quite a vampire yet. If he was a full vampire, the stake would have gone in before the burial.

The more logical legend of Teodor Glava, which fits with the plot of Bram Stoker's fictional *Dracula* and most Hollywood movies on the topic, goes like this:

It is said that in the winter of 1918, some Lafayetters were suspicious of Canfieldians, due to the string of mysterious—some say demonic—thefts the previous summer, all occurring on Tuesday nights and only at houses with porch swings. Canfield was a small coal camp about three miles north of Lafayette and one mile west of Erie, near Boulder Creek. One Canfield victim, Mrs. Brown, awoke one Monday morning to find that her screen door was still in place but missing the hinges, closing spring and handle. There it was, just sitting in the doorframe by itself. She touched it and—bam!—it fell over and hit the floor. The next weekend, Mr. Wise, of Wise Homestead notoriety, found his porch swing flat on the front porch with no sign of the chains or hooks to hold it up to the porch ceiling. (Legend has it that people being afraid of their porch swing hardware disappearing is the reason you don't see a lot of porch swings in Lafayette to this very day.)

Knowing that Dracula was able to manipulate hardware by being able to lock and unlock doors using telekinetic powers—as Jonathan Harker encounters in Dracula's castle—Canfield residents feared the worst: The demon himself, or some bloodthirsty minion, was loose and wreaking hardware havoc.

Word spread quickly to neighboring Lafayette: Be on the lookout for Dracula! Several locals, particularly immigrant and migrant coal miners—from faraway lands such as Italy, Bulgaria and Missouri—living along Lafayette's Gooseberry Gulch sprang into action, sprinkling holy water on their front door handles and hinges. Concurrently, Old Town residents heard mumblings of an immigrant named Glava, a visitor from Canfield who during the winter months shopped for his coal mining supplies in Lafayette only after the sun went down. He frequently appeared to be "under the weather." Aha, thought the locals: It must be a vampire!

On an early December morning, word spread that Glava may have faked his death to escape scrutiny. Undertaker R.R. Powell assured locals that Glava had in fact died and insisted that a graveside ceremony would take place despite six inches of snow at the cemetery.

Town employee Sam Carlisle ordinarily spent his weekdays maintaining the dirt streets and sweeping the wood plank sidewalks. But due to the uptick in deaths as a result of the Spanish flu pandemic, Carlisle was tasked with digging graves at the Lafayette Cemetery. And they all had to be dug by hand. Glava's grave was dug on Thursday for the Friday burial. Because it was one of the snowiest months on record—Denver received 19.6 inches of snow in December 1918—Carlisle was tasked with first clearing 6.0 inches of snow from the grave, then he toiled with a pickax through 2.0 feet of frozen ground before the digging got easier. The pile of dirt from the six-foot grave was covered with tattered remnants of brattice cloth so that the warm soil could thaw the frozen dirt. This would make it easier to shovel the dirt back into the hole the next day, after the ceremony.

Although gatherings were forbidden by a quarantine order, a large group of nonresidents met for Glava's morning graveside ceremony. Legend has it that they, too, looked "under the weather." Sam was also there but stayed in the background and was thinking only of getting the casket covered before the dirt pile froze. The ceremony ended, the suspicious-looking mourners dispersed and Sam backfilled the grave.

But the strange, pale man being dead and buried didn't quell the local population's hardware anxieties. They didn't want their doors disturbed! Defying the quarantine orders and armed against ghostly as well as mortal attack—two moldy cloves of dried garlic from Mrs. Livnik's root cellar, two small crucifixes, three large ones, one shotgun, a pistol, two pitchforks, three shovels, a bowie knife like the one that killed Dracula and a mortise lock and a hasp, both of which were blessed by Father Patrick—a large mob the size of a small mob set out from Gooseberry Gulch and arrived at the Lafayette Cemetery about 2:00 p.m., two hours after Glava's grave had been filled. After spending two hours uncovering six feet of dirt, and with about an hour of daylight to spare, the casket lid was lifted and the hardware heathen was staked in the heart with the fallen branch of a nearby elm tree that had been whittled to a point and decorated with smiley faces while the crowd waited two hours for the dirt to be removed.

As insurance and to prevent Glava from walking the physical world as an undead monster, the band of vampire killers placed a stem from a Harison's wild yellow rosebush on top of the closed coffin to trap the vampire for an eternity. (Legend has it that the wild rose grew into the yellow rosebush at the head of Glava's grave and the stake from the elm tree grew into the juniper tree.) The vampire killers did have the sensibility to backfill the grave a second time so that Sam Carlisle didn't have to do it.

Not having fully read the litany of Old World instructions on how to properly dispatch the undead, particularly a vampire, the Gooseberry Gulch gang had failed to cut off Glava's head and place garlic in its mouth. Because of that, the body's in a liminal state and not fully "dead," and Glava's restless corpse must endure eternity in a double-secret, semi-vampire purgatory where he's kind of like Schrödinger's vampire cat: He's both undead and dead.

Sixty years later, and because none of the novice vampire killers' preventive measures have worked, it is said that friends of best friends are reporting an average-height, medium-build figure with long fingernails and a red Canfield Ace Hardware shirt sitting on the grave and walking about the cemetery. Alternatively, it is said, the limited preventive measures worked and the still-buried, kinda, sorta vampire Glava, angry about the whole matter, expresses his anger by making the temperature of the flat headstone subzero, which is where Yeti got the idea for the square blue Yeti Ice freezing blocks for the company's outrageously expensive coolers.

# 3
# LOUISVILLE'S BOOTLEGGER GHOSTS

As part of a 2016 Louisville get-together, a Denver-based ghost-hunting group shared online the eerie narrative of the ghosts haunting the Melting Pot restaurant at 732 Main Street in Louisville. The ghost-hunting narrative, fit for any prime-time cable channel, cites a legend that the mining tunnels under Main Street were used by Prohibition-era (1916–33 in Colorado) bootleggers to distill and sell alcohol and to travel to and from the scattered speakeasies. According to legend, a still exploded in the tunnel under the Melting Pot, killing three bootleggers. They were buried in the explosion, so the story goes, and it took workers several days to reach the bodies. Two bodies were recovered; third was never found, "it is said."

Fast-forward to the year 2000 and beyond, and ghost hunters' tales of apparitions of the noisy, drunken "third bootlegger" abound. And not only in and around the Melting Pot, the ghost hunters say, but also in "different locations on Main Street."

The narrative continues: "It is also rumored that the original mine was built on sacred Native American burial grounds, and in moving the shaft, the owner of the restaurant had disturbed angry spirits. The mine shaft was re-erected and the restaurant did open, but met with one mysterious mishap after another. Screws in support beams disappeared, the roof collapsed twice, and breaker boxes kept short-circuiting. According to the paranormal experts, both ghosts of the Native Americans and the old bootlegger now reside in the building.

The Melting Pot restaurant in Louisville with the reconstructed mine tipple imported from Madrid, New Mexico. The former Black Diamond Saloon is the site of numerous ghost sightings, starting in the 1990s. *Photo by the author, 2023.*

"Employees say they hear sounds of a 'drunken old man' yelling and knocking over pots and pans. The ghosts from New Mexico reside in the mineshaft that towers over the downtown area. Spiritualists who have made contact with the ghosts say the spirits only wish to view the mountain range and to look south towards their homeland."

The ghost tale at the Melting Pot takes on the trajectory of the Lafayette Vampire tale: Bits and pieces of it (the generations-old Prohibition tunnels myth) are traded among schoolchildren for decades, then—simultaneous with the growing popularity of the internet and the launch of a new restaurant—the legend gains "enhancements" and grows by leaps and bounds, crammed with historical "facts" that could not possibly be valid.

In 2020, a video was posted on the Melting Pot's official Facebook page, "Haunting Investigations: The Melting Pot of Louisville, Colorado." The creator of the video is neither revealed nor credited, but the video's narrator strikes a familiar "let's make things up" narrative, accompanied with historical coal mining photographs from Gary, West Virginia; Hot Springs, Arkansas; and Midlothian, Virginia.

The video narrative continues: "According to legend, a tragedy occurred in the tunnel directly under the building that currently houses the Melting

Circa 1950 photo of the false front Mangus Building that formerly occupied 732 Main Street in Louisville. It was subsumed by the Black Diamond Saloon building in 1984. No historical photographs or maps show any kind of structure on the vacant north half of the lot. *Courtesy Louisville Historical Museum.*

Pot restaurant. A still exploded in the tunnel killing three bootleggers and sealing the shaft. Because of the danger in the damaged shaft, it took rescuers days to exhume two of the bodies. The third was never found. Apparitions of the third bootlegger have been witnessed ever since. Some of the staff members refer to him as 'Joey.'"

The video describes staff hearing footsteps, seeing apparitions of a ghostly figure and seeing glasses being thrown across the room with no one around. In an interview in the video, Samantha Williams, the restaurant's manager, details seeing—out of the corner of her eye—a wine glass in the bar area flying across the room and shattering.

## WHOA, WHOA. HOLD ON A SEC

Pausing for a moment to dissect the internet-based fiction, three inconsistencies rise to the top.

First, the Melting Pot building was remodeled in the mid-1980s by restaurateur Rick Ross, who reassembled the massive timber mine tipple (not a "shaft" or "mine") brought from Madrid, New Mexico. A mine tipple is the dominant aboveground structure, shaped like an "A," that was used in local coal mines to haul coal cars and miners up and down the mine's main shaft. During the area's peak of coal mining, roughly 1905 to 1910, dozens of massive tipples dotted the east Boulder County landscape. At the time the tipple was installed, Ross told the Broomfield weekly newspaper, some of the timbers were four hundred years old.

Prior to the tipple reconstruction project at 732 Main Street, a nondescript, one-story storefront housed Señor T's, a terrific Mexican restaurant ably owned and managed by Ted and Carolyn Manzanares. Señor T's moved across Main Street about 1975, and Rick opened his Black Diamond Restaurant in the former Señor T's building in 1981. He later expanded into a total of six thousand square feet of restaurant space and anchored his delicious menu with one of the best hamburgers the town has ever known.

Prior to Señor T's and Black Diamond, the original nine-hundred-square-foot wood structure was historically known as the Mangus Building. In 1897, about the time it was built, it was known as "Pappy" Clark's store. Louisville pioneer "Uncle" David Kerr owned the building in the early 1900s, and the Mayhoffer family (spelled "Mayrhofer" back then) had ownership before that. After the Manguses bought the building in 1927, it housed Christie's Red and White store, a chain grocery store. It then housed the following establishments: Johnnie's Red and White Store (until 1942), Boyd Green's Red and White, Varra's Red and White Food Store, Louisville Cleaners, Ye Olde Donut Shoppe, Louisville Flower and Gift Shop, Señor T's, BB's Delicatessen and Black Diamond. Flora Mangus sold the building to Rick Ross in 1981. There is no evidence that the building housed a bar, saloon, pool hall or food service establishment prior to the donut shop.

Boulder County clerk and recorder records from 1948 state that 732 Main Street was built in 1900, although 1893 and 1900 Sanborn Fire Insurance maps show a smaller, seven-hundred-square-foot building sitting about ten feet back from the sidewalk. The north half of the lot is vacant. Photos from 1948 and 1955 show a building with the same width but the windows and doors of the false front hug the sidewalk. So a false front was added to the original gable building, but the remodel date is uncertain.

Rick Ross said in a 2023 interview with me that the old Red and White building—the Mangus Building—had no basement, just a crawlspace under the rear portion of the structure. "It for sure wasn't tall enough to stand up

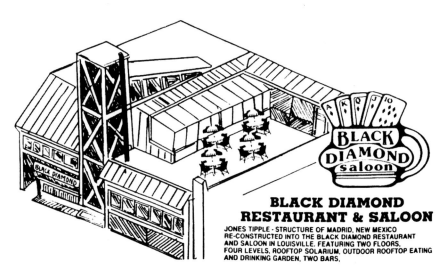

BLACK DIAMOND
RESTAURANT & SALOON
JONES TIPPLE - STRUCTURE OF MADRID, NEW MEXICO
RE-CONSTRUCTED INTO THE BLACK DIAMOND RESTAURANT
AND SALOON IN LOUISVILLE. FEATURING TWO FLOORS,
FOUR LEVELS, ROOFTOP SOLARIUM, OUTDOOR ROOFTOP EATING
AND DRINKING GARDEN, TWO BARS,

Illustration of the Black Diamond Saloon, circa 1987. *Courtesy Rick Ross.*

in," said Ross. In 1984, he excavated and poured a new, larger foundation for the restaurant expansion but left the original building's foundation largely intact. Neither the new foundation nor the old crawlspace revealed any evidence whatsoever of any type of tunnel or tunnel access. There was also no trace of disturbed soil in the north portion of the new building, formerly the vacant portion of the lot.

Ross, the person who acquired and reassembled the New Mexico mine tipple, said in the same interview that nothing out of the ordinary occurred at the restaurant, to him or anyone who worked there, during the eight years he operated it (1981–89). Nothing happened before, during or after the tipple was built. No Native American elders gave him any warnings. There were no mysterious mishaps—a roof collapse or missing parts. No contractors or their employees were afraid to work, and there were no experiences with or sightings of ghosts or apparitions. There were no flying objects and no unusual noises (footsteps, crashing pans, people whispering). No nothing.

Ross did say in 2023 that during the 1980s' expansion he left a "few surprises" hidden in the walls behind drywall, like initials carved into the backsides of the timbers—the types of surprises that will likely become part of a ghost legend generations from now.

So the origin of the Melting Pot legend—and the propagation of its tantalizing details of the third bootlegger ghost and the disturbed Native American spirits—started after 1989 and weren't and aren't a part of any long-standing legend forwarded by anyone local. Still, we're treated to the old "according to legend" shtick.

The legend of speakeasy tunnels? Yes, that's local myth and part of long-standing Louisville legend. Bootleggers using them and dying in them? No, that's not part of long-standing Louisville legend.

Second, the coal seams under downtown worked by the Acme coal mine until 1928 ranged from seventy to two hundred feet deep. This means that any mine tunnels, known as passageways and entries, were well belowground. Coal was removed from the Acme Mine from 1890 until 1928, and the mine was idle between 1910 and 1917.

Active mine or not, the stupidity of hauling barrels of tunnel-made hooch a half mile through underground tunnels, then up a non-operational, eighteen-story central mine shaft is outdone only by the stupidity of lighting and operating the still's open flame in a coal mine tunnel (or any other type of underground tunnel) potentially filled with methane.

More significantly, the Acme Mine's tunnels were not accessible from the surface (except from the main shaft) or from any basement in any building in Louisville.

Technically, the legend states that the mine shaft used by the bootleggers was at the Melting Pot, which would have been impossible, because the shaft-sinking process involves dynamite. A small group of lawbreakers— even Mafia-backed lawbreakers—would not have had the expertise, time, energy, materials, money or guts to sink their own mine shaft. (The State of Colorado coal inspectors charged with regulating mines mention in 1905 that a Lafayette coal mine was able to sink a shaft at the rate of four feet per day. This included dozens of men using explosives, a large bucket lift to remove the fractured shale and clay, some railway mechanism to move the excavated dirt from the shaft to another location and railcar loads of timber to shore it up. Even with state-of-the-art equipment, a shaft under the Melting Pot would have taken several months to complete, dozens of men and thousands of dollars. All for the sake of an illegal still that makes twenty or thirty gallons a day? I don't think so.)

It would have been much easier and safer to distill whiskey on the surface and in, say, the basement of your house.

Oddly enough, Louisville businessman Mike Colacci of Blue Parrot restaurant fame did make whiskey during Prohibition—a scheme called the "Coal Mine Still." In the 2004 book *Louisville Legends: The Record as History*, Joe Colacci (the "unidentified source" described in the book) recounts his dad's bootlegging adventures, which included placing barrels of whiskey in a truck at a coal mine east of Louisville, then loading coal in the truck to hide the hooch. The truck, illegal whiskey and coal then made their way to Omaha, Nebraska.

Boulder County newspapers detail dozens of sheriff's raids from 1900 to 1935 at locations in Louisville. Raids made at saloons and pool halls usually involved illegal gambling, not illegal liquor or prostitution. The county sheriff's liquor raids made in Louisville during Prohibition mostly involved bootleggers making beer, wine and whiskey in their homes, usually in the basement. In September 1924, the sheriff raided James "Jim" Colacci's house on Main Street and hauled away an illegal still capable of producing fifty gallons of whiskey. Mike and Jim Colacci were brothers, although it's not known if Mike's bootlegging and Jim's bootlegging were one and the same. (It was probably the case but is not known for sure. And it's important to note that although Mike Colacci was arrested in 1922 for serving illegal whiskey at his own Blue Parrot restaurant, most of the product didn't stay in Louisville. It went to Nebraska.)

Although there are only a handful of copies of the weekly *Louisville Times* from the early 1900s—the file copies were discarded after W.S. Withers bought the newspaper in 1931—it's possible to research and track mine (and tunnel) explosions and tragedies in Louisville using both the *Denver Post* and *Rocky Mountain News* archives. And a deep dive into those archives brings up a big goose egg. No stories about stills exploding or Prohibition tunnels caving in or bootleggers killed or unrecovered bodies. And a tragedy of that scale—three people killed and an unrecovered body—would have made the front pages.

Third, the Native American portion of the ghost hunters' narrative is problematic. If Native American spirits were indeed peeved about a tipple being built on their sacred New Mexico grounds, they'd be happier than heck to see it disassembled and sent elsewhere. If they did hitch a ride on the tipple parts and pieces (maybe out of spite?), imagine how peeved they'll be one hundred or more years from now when the building's torn down, hauled to the landfill and then buried. (That landfill's in for big trouble.)

## GHOSTS? COULD BE

OK, OK, I give up. Maybe there were ghosts at the Melting Pot who popped out of nowhere in the 1990s, but they're not who the paranormal investigators claim. These restless souls trapped in purgatory were more likely among the men killed in the Acme Mine.

The main shaft of the Acme coal mine, the access point to the mine tunnels, was one-half mile south of 732 Main Street, but a network of the mine's passageways existed under most of Old Town. No coal company maps of the Acme show an access shaft or air shaft near 732 Main Street. (State mining officials concluded in the early 1990s that 90 percent of the coal mine tunnels in east Boulder County had collapsed over the years, meaning there are no remaining voids. So relax. Nothing at the surface is collapsing anytime soon.)

Actual deaths at the Acme Mine from 1888 to 1928, when it closed, as reported by the *Lafayette News*, *Rocky Mountain News*, *Daily Camera*, Boulder County coroner records, the Louisville Historical Museum's "The Louisville Historian" and other sources include the following:

May 18, 1891: "Coal Miner Named Isaacs," killed by falling rock

December 28, 1892: George McIvor (McIver) and "16-year-old boy named Ransom" hanged by the hoist rope when they tried to clear a stuck lift according to the newspaper, although the state coal inspector reported that they were crushed between the lift and the wall of the shaft

February 22, 1894: Frank Stock, died of ceiling cave-in

March 27, 1895: Jacob Gearnick (or Chamack), crushed by rock while pushing mine car underground

April 4, 1900: James Craig, suicide by jumping down main shaft

November 26, 1907: August Risetti, fell 180 feet into open mouth of shaft

January 9, 1920: Jack Smith, died after being crushed by coal car

March 10, 1926: John Stritz (or Stretz), died of injuries from January 1926 lift accident

February 4, 1928: William Kirk, died from cave-in

# 4

# LA LLORONA AND OTHER LEGENDARY SPIRITS

*Legend has it that the ghost woman we know as La Llorona travels at night from place to place, sometimes on a white horse and sometimes on a black horse. She is torn between good and bad—in other words, between Satan the Devil and God. Her soul or spirit is never at rest. She cries out at night in a sound of complete terror to please help her to put her soul to rest. Many of the New Mexico old-timers claim, in fact, that they have seen her sitting on her horse in very remote places in northern New Mexico, mainly around rivers, streams, creeks and even dry arroyos, in her white robe, swinging a sword or whip and screeching very loud in a blood-curdling sound for you to follow her and she would lead you from the Devil and back to the Church. This would be the good side of her spirit. On the bad side she might curse and ask you to follow her to Hell, where she felt her soul might be resting. In short her soul was lost and she was seeking same—it was in Heaven or Hell.*
—*George O. Tate, Espanola, New Mexico,* La Llorona: Encounters with the Weeping Woman *(2022)*

M ike Romero, mayor of Lafayette from 1994 to 1995, introduced La Llorona to readers of the *Lafayette News* in 1995. He used the La Llorona legend to illustrate how neighbors should look out for one another, even when the threat is imagined.

"La Llorona is searching for the babies she drowned many years ago. The crying woman (llorona) is found in most every Spanish-speaking community in the Southwest. I am sure stories go back into the 1800s," wrote Romero.

La Llorona of Mexican mythology. *Illustration courtesy ViCee25 via Wikimedia Commons.*

"The first action I took [to defend myself against La Llorona] was to wear a cross, a medal of St. Christopher and to recite a prayer from a prayer card I earned as Catechism. This was effective for a time. But at some point, I was able to discern what was dangerous or what was just an overactive imagination. For one thing, I knew all the neighbors, so there were safe haven options open to me. The message my brothers and I got was that there was REAL DANGER out there and there is security at home."

Just as teenagers dared one another to visit the Lafayette Cemetery at night, they also ventured into the remote perimeters of Old Town Lafayette to confront the legendary La Llorona, who reportedly kidnapped and killed both curious children and curious adults. The legendary crying woman was either next to Coal Creek, or somewhere along the railroad tracks. A local variation of the legend was that La Llorona walking the railroad tracks carried in her arms the severed head of her child.

Among the favorite places for a chance encounter was the old city dump along Coal Creek, now Flagg Park (where Flagg Drive turns north toward Highway 7). The Burlington Northern railroad tracks that hugged the east edge of Lafayette's Old Town was the other likely place to find La Llorona.

If young La Llorona hunters did encounter the apparition on the railroad tracks, one defense used locally was to place a knife on the tracks. This defensive mechanism to ward off a spirit is rooted in the Sihuanaba, a supernatural being from Central American folklore similar to La Llorona. Biting a machete was the preferred method of warding off the Sihuanaba.

"My friends and I bicycled to the top of the hill east of Lafayette and heard this wailing sound down by the creek, like someone crying," said Frank Archuleta in 2023. "We walked down towards Coal Creek and saw this white object suspended in the air and moving along the creek. Same thing happened two years later [on the mesa above Coal Creek at 120th and

Coal Creek near Flagg Park in east Lafayette, where Lafayette kids often ventured in search of La Llorona. *Photo by the author, 2023.*

Dillon Road] but with no wailing. Just a mysterious white object floating above the field."

The story of La Llorona originated in Central America in the time of the conquistadors and the conquest of Mexico. La Llorona was a young woman who fathered a child with a white man. After being abandoned by the man, she throws the child into the river. She tries to rescue the child, but it's too late. Overcome by remorse, she goes mad, and her crying or screaming soul is doomed to wander eternally.

It's a centuries-old lesson on moral and social cohesion (i.e., stay at home so you don't get into trouble) and a warning of how to behave appropriately as a mother (i.e., don't murder your children).

# THE OLD LOUISVILLE INN GHOST AND OTHER LOUISVILLE HAUNTINGS

This ghost tale, centered on the Old Louisville Inn at 740 Front Street in Louisville, is similar to the Melting Pot ghost tale, as it involves a generations-old legend that won't die: Prohibition-era speakeasies in Louisville were connected by tunnels fashioned by coal miners in their leisure time. Bar and speakeasy patrons, it is said, used the tunnels to escape sheriff raids and to dodge nosey wives hunting for perfidious spouses.

The legend of Prohibition tunnels and ghosts at Old Louisville Inn gained prominence in 1994, when an ambitious restaurateur purchased and renovated the bar and restaurant at 740 Front Street. His and other long-standing tunnel legends don't pinpoint exact tunnel connections, with the exception that one Prohibition tunnel went from the building that housed Colacci's restaurant to the building across the street that housed Pasquale's bar. Scores of longtime Louisville residents have a tunnel tale—heard from a grandfather, father, uncle or aunt—describing a plethora of tunnels going from the Blue Parrot on Pine Street to various places, from the Old Louisville Inn on Front Street to various places, from the former Louisville High School building on north Main Street to various places, from…well, you get the idea. There's even a legend that the train stopped and unloaded bootleg booze at the Old Louisville Inn, which was the tunnel system's central hub or distribution point.

The Front Street restaurateur showed the "tunnel entrances" to me a few years after his purchase, and the evidence was underwhelming. The "tunnels" in the basement appeared to me to be newer brick and mortar repairs to the foundation. Nothing more, nothing less.

The former Old Louisville Inn, now the restaurant 740 Front, at 740 Front Street in Louisville. *Photo by the author, 2023.*

Circa 1970s photo of the Old Louisville Inn, where stories of ghosts abound. *Courtesy Louisville Historical Museum.*

As was the case with the "big reveal," no one—Louisville resident or otherwise—has produced physical evidence of a Prohibition tunnel. There are no photos and no firsthand accounts of constructing it or walking through it. (Was it large or small? Narrow or wide? Shallow or deep underground?). There are no maps or drawings showing locations and directions, no pieces of timbers or rusted hardware from a collapsed tunnel buried in the ground and no confirmation of a tunnel—not even any disturbed soil—from several public works projects that removed and replaced substantial amounts of soil along the entire length and breadth of Main Street.

The only firsthand tunnel sighting that I am aware of involves Mary (Colacci) Geyer, a family friend of mine, who said she witnessed her father, Tony Colacci (founder of Colacci's restaurant on Main Street), seal up an entrance "to a tunnel" that Geyer said ran under the street from Colacci's at 816 Main Street to Pasquale's across the street at 817 Main. But it's likely that Mary was viewing a long-since filled-in coal chute on the Main Street side of the building.

But this is a book about legends, ghosts and other worldly encounters (and, if needed, debunking the aforementioned). So a comprehensive debunking of the myth of Louisville tunnels will have to wait for its own book.

Speaking of debunking, the tale of a ghost named Samantha haunting Old Louisville Inn, now 740 Front restaurant, was launched prior to 1992 by Hugh and Virginia McKenzie, former restaurateurs who owned the building from 1973 to 1992. They named the made-up ghost after Elizabeth Montgomery's character on the television series *Bewitched*. Post-1992 enhancements to the McKenzies' invented legend include Samantha being an early-1900s prostitute who worked in the brothel in a back room of the saloon.

Unfortunately, there's no historical evidence that the building housed a brothel, nor is there any evidence that Front Street was a "Red Light District." (Factually, the demolished Hecla Mine casino located northeast of Louisville was used as a brothel. And in a 1998 *Louisville Times* article, the late Mary (DiGiacomo) Poydock remembered "Ladies of the Night" living next door to her house, which wasn't on Front Street.)

But the saloons weren't squeaky clean. In April 1909, the *Longmont Ledger* reported that Boulder County sheriff M.P. Capp raided a Louisville saloon and seized "gambling paraphernalia." In August of that same year, Capp raided twenty saloons across Boulder County and seized a slot machine from a Louisville saloon operator. The saloon owners were arrested, but not the patrons. In March 1935, the county sheriff raided a Louisville pool hall for illegal gambling and arrested twenty men. (Twenty men arrested? I thought there were tunnels so they wouldn't get caught! By the way, in an exhaustive search of 150 years of newspaper articles at coloradohistoricnewspapers. org dealing with sheriffs' and revenuers' raids at Louisville saloons and pool halls, none of the dozens of stories say, "The sheriff raided a Louisville pool hall Friday night and, mysteriously, all the patrons had disappeared.")

Most significantly with the Old Louisville Inn ghost tale, any notion that a prostitute was killed by a customer in the basement of 740 Front Street is pure fabrication, because Samantha the prostitute ghost was created as a joke in order to scare kitchen staff. (Ghost? Maybe. Ghost of a former prostitute? Nope.)

Unfortunately, this hasn't stopped Denver TV stations and travel blogs from reporting and writing about the "haunting." In 2017, the blog *Travel Boulder* (travelboulder.com) placed Old Louisville Inn on its list of "Most Haunted Places."

"Head to the attic if you want to feel or hear the spirits that supposedly live in this restaurant," the blog advised. "People have claimed to hear strange voices and mysterious coughing. Other people have said they

"Ichabod Pursued by the Headless Horseman," by F.O.C. Darley, from *Le Magasin Pittoresque*, 1849. *Wikimedia Commons, public domain.*

see a disembodied hand running the cash register and have felt a ghost in the room."

Are there any attributable accounts of strange things happening at the Old Louisville Inn? Sure.

Dawn (Anspach) Treasure, a Lafayette resident who worked for several years at the inn, recalls sitting at the bar after a shift and just after closing, when a loud crashing sound was heard in the kitchen. Investigating, workers found no one in the kitchen but discovered that a large baking sheet had been flung across the kitchen.

# The Headless Guy

Longtime Louisville resident Shelley (Caranci) Angell reminded me of a legend kids passed around in the 1960s of the Headless Horseman haunting Spruce Lane, a dirt road on the western outskirts of Old Town Louisville.

Similar to the "hey kids, stay close to home" lesson of La Llorona, the myth of the Headless Horseman has been retold around the world since the Middle Ages. In American folklore, the marauding demon—the restless soul of a Hessian soldier who lost his head in battle—appeared in the short story "The Legend of Sleepy Hollow," published in 1820.

In adulthood and while director of the Louisville Chamber of Commerce, Angell described a friendly ghost that would relocate and rearrange office items in the chamber's Main Street office. A sponsorship sign for a chamber event, which neither she nor administrative assistant Lani Melvin could find, appeared one day propped up on a chair around the conference table. "We looked for that sign for weeks and couldn't find it. Then it just showed up," said Angell. "We laughed and laughed about our friendly ghost helping us out."

Joan (Colacci) Riggins remembers a tale from her childhood about a witch living under the railroad tracks next to Main Street near South Boulder Road. Yes, there's still a culvert running under the tracks. I dunno, could still be a witch there.

# 6
# The Neighborhood Ghost and Other Lafayette Hauntings

The house at 301 West Cleveland in Lafayette that Tarey and Dawn (Anspach) Treasure own has been in the Anspach family since Dawn's dad and mom, Glen and Dee Anspach, bought it in 1964. A beautiful two-story Victorian built in 1910, it was one of the first handful of homes to be erected on the west side of Public Road in the Mountain View subdivision.

In my research of the home's history via county clerk and *Lafayette News* archives, the property doesn't have any death or tragedy of particular significance. Since there weren't nearby hospitals or hospice care facilities, it was common for people to pass away in their own homes. That happened all over town. But Dawn's older brother, Graig Anspach, did hear from a neighbor that a former owner had hanged himself in the house.

Dawn has lived in the home for all but ten years of the family's ownership. After Glen's death in 1983, Dawn's mom, Dee, kept up the household by herself. Dee moved to a retirement community in 2005, and Tarey and Dawn decided to move into the house and started renovations in 2006.

Tarey and Dawn have in their house what they describe as a friendly ghost. "Mischievous but friendly," they say. For Dawn, encounters with the spirit started about 1993, when Dawn's daughter Aimee opened the front door to come in with no one home and heard the distinct sound of dishes clattering, as if they were being cleaned and placed in a drying rack. In examining the kitchen, Aimee didn't see any sign of dishes being cleaned nor any dishes even out of the cupboards.

*Left*: The Treasure/ Anspach house at 301 West Cleveland in Lafayette. Numerous encounters with ghosts were detailed between 1964 and 2022. *Photo by the author, 2023.*

*Below*: A 1960 photo of 301 West Cleveland in Lafayette. *Courtesy Boulder County Clerk and Recorder.*

The next encounters with the ghost or spirit were in evening hours during the 2006 renovation of the home. Tarey often worked alone while rehabbing the second floor, work that involved stripping wallpaper, removing and refinishing doors and door trim and refurbishing crown mouldings at the ceiling. Several times during the work, Tarey would hear a female voice softly say his name. On several occasions, he repeatedly heard, "Tarey, Tarey," and would search upstairs and downstairs rooms and open the front door to see if anyone was outside. He found nothing.

"One night I was heading home [from the West Cleveland renovation], when I opened the front door and got ready to close and lock it from outside," said Tarey in a 2022 interview with me. "No sooner than I'd put the key in I felt a strong pull to the door handle from the inside, as if someone or something didn't want the door to close." Again, Tarey found nothing.

On one occasion, a power sander turned on by itself. Tarey said, "I unplugged it and got the heck out of there...and didn't return to the house for several weeks."

The most confounding encounter happened when Tarey was redoing the upstairs crown moulding. That process involved removing the intricately mitered pieces, stripping them and finishing them, then nailing the labeled pieces back to their original places. "I'd renailed all of the pieces—some very long pieces—so that they looked like they'd always been there, but noticed the last piece, a small piece, was missing," said Tarey. "It had been there—I'd readied it for nailing—but then it wasn't there. I looked and looked but couldn't find it."

Two weeks later, on entering the house one morning, Tarey found the small refinished piece of trim upstairs, propped against a wall.

Tarey and Dawn's combined households from previous marriages included children Andy, Ashlie, Aimee, Jennifer and Delain. The couple's grandsons Trystian and Jaiden joined the family in Lafayette after Tarey's daughter, Jennifer, was killed in a traffic accident.

After Trystian moved into the house in 2010, the couple noticed that the three-year-old would often stare out the front window and say, "Ghost not get me." Trystian would sometimes mention the ghost while sitting on the couch in the family room and watching TV.

The couple thought at the time that this was odd behavior, as the two had never mentioned or talked about the ghost around Trystian. In addition to Trystian's sightings, the couple would notice subdued flashes of light out of the corners of their eyes. "Like car headlight reflections, only there was no traffic on the street," said Dawn.

Anspach's Jewelry at 101 South Public Road in Lafayette, the site of many mysterious happenings. *Photo by the author, 2023.*

A 1948 photo of 101 South Public Road in Lafayette, which housed the Bluebird Cafe and Lounge. *Courtesy Boulder County Clerk and Recorder.*

Around the same time, sounds of footsteps on the upstairs floor and of doors closing were common occurrences. The couple's two dogs never barked but would stare up the stairwell.

Encounters with the spirit subsided over time but recurred in 2022 after a Wi-Fi doorbell with a video camera was installed next to the front door. Tarey recalls the doorbell ringing and the door opening on its own, but after investigating, Tarey found no one at the door and no evidence on recorded video of anyone ringing the doorbell.

# THE TRAVELING GHOST?

A few blocks from Tarey and Dawn Treasure's house, Dawn's older brother Graig Anspach had his own ghost stories to tell.

During the gut renovation of Anspach's Jewelry in January 2023, Graig started hearing strange noises while working after closing time in the part of the store that wasn't being renovated. The sound was of people dancing and the chatter of bar patrons having a good time.

The building housing Anspach's Jewelry is at 101 South Public Road and was erected about 1900 by Peter Peltier. It was formerly the Elkhorn Saloon, among the first saloons in Lafayette. Peltier built the structure a few lots south of 101 South Public and later (between 1902 and 1908) moved it north. A lean-to structure was added, and Graig said it was probably a livery stable and then a car repair garage. The lean-to was converted into the dance hall portion of the Blue Bird Cafe and Tavern (Bagdonas' Cafe), later Mauro's Restaurant and Lounge. During Lafayette's early years, all of the saloons were sequestered along the "wet side" of Lafayette, a two-block segment of the west side of Public Road at Simpson Street. Anspach's dad and mom, Glen and Dee, moved their jewelry shop to 101 South Public Road in 1967.

Anspach acknowledges that the barroom dancing noises could be clatter from Public Road car traffic, but it doesn't explain the chatter of bar patrons. And the host of previous encounters he's had with spirits in the storefront went beyond strange noises. Those encounters almost always involved a second witness who experienced the same oddity.

Unexplained movements of furniture and display jewelry started about 2013, when Anspach's nephew Delain Treasure started working at the store. At the time, Delain was living at 301 West Cleveland Street.

"My other nephew who worked with me, Ty, and I were hanging out after work, and we witnessed a half-filled gallon paint can cartwheel off a storage shelf, and land upright," said Anspach. "It was heavy, and there's no way it just casually fell off the shelf. Shortly after that occurrence, we were doing the same thing—just hanging out after the store closed—and a swivel chair from the watch repair work station rolled backwards from the desk, rotated 180 degrees to the left, then 180 degrees to the right, then rolled back to its original place."

On several occasions, Anspach and others working in the store witnessed jewelry chain displays tumbling off of shelves. Anspach said the displays are designed so that if they fall on their own, they slide bottom first. All of the displays tumbled top first and resulted in display pieces "all over the floor."

"We never felt threatened or scared by any of it," said Anspach. "It was more amusing and mischievous, as if the ghost or spirit was having fun rather than trying to spook us."

Is it possible that the same ghost traveled from the house he grew up in to Anspach's place of business and back? He said it was possible, because the same sorts of mysterious and mischievous encounters on Cleveland Street happened at the store as well.

Wait. He had encounters at the Anspach house, too?

Sure enough, when Anspach was about six years old (about 1964), he often rooted around the basement of his boyhood home at 301 West Cleveland. It had a dug-out basement with an outdoor entrance, but he often explored the crawlspace area in search of bottles and other belongings left by previous occupants.

"One day, I left the access door open, but while I was hanging out, the outside hatch slammed shut and the [hook and eye] latch somehow engaged and locked me down there," said Anspach. "I yelled and yelled for help for a couple hours before my mom heard me and came and unlatched the door so I could get out."

About four years later, Anspach was home alone and set about the evening routine of pulling into place the roller window shades in the living room. "As I was coming back to the living room from the kitchen," said Anspach, "all of the shades on all of the downstairs windows—there were eight—rolled back up at the same time. There were always the typical stairs and floor creaking sounds at night, just like in most old houses, but the shades flying up was unusual.

"We never talked about our friendly ghost in the sense of having a family meeting and saying 'Hey, did you see the ghost?' For me, the experiences were just, 'That was weird and amusing but let's move on.'"

# THE LAFAYETTE HOUSE

Rachel Hanson and her husband, Jeremy, own and reside in the Lafayette House, at 600 East Simpson Street. The building was among the first structures erected in Lafayette and was a hotel (Lafayette House, Bryant Hotel, Union Hotel) and later a boardinghouse for miners working at the nearby Simpson Mine. In the 1940s and '50s, it was used as an elementary school as part of the Pillar of Fire Church.

The building has the most potential for hauntings, and it kinda, sorta makes the grade.

When renters occupied the building, Hansons heard about one tenant having to hire a Catholic priest to exorcise a spirit. And the mother of another tenant felt the presence of the spirit of a small child, the victim of a drowning, inhabiting a stairway.

Both of these "events" were news to the Hansons, who haven't experienced anything unusual since converting it to their own residence.

The Hansons did find a blue-black dress during exterior renovations tucked into the floor joists of the upper level. It's hard to determine the age of the mystery dress, but Rachel cleaned the plaster from it, hand-

Circa 1910 photo of the Lafayette House at 600 East Simpson Street in Lafayette. *Courtesy Lafayette History Museum, Lafayette Historical Society.*

laundered it and wore it as a Halloween costume. (Was it the 1890s black dress used to haunt the house along Coal Creek described in earlier chapters? Probably not.)

## ENTERTAINMENT FOR THE WEDDING PARTY

Lafayette's least-publicized palace of paranormal proclivities, including a "portal to the underworld," is the Dove House and Lionsgate Events Center at 1055 U.S. 287 in south Lafayette, across from Good Samaritan Medical Center. Employees have heard mysterious footsteps and experienced lights flickering, and guests have seen the apparition of an elderly woman in a nightgown on a staircase. One employee at the wedding venue was mopping the floor when bare footprints of children running appeared on the floor in the mop water.

In her 2020 *What's Her Name* podcast, described earlier in this book, host Olivia Meikle details a paranormal investigation at the events center involving the ghost of a little boy. The investigators placed numerous balls on the floor and taped them to the floor to see if the ghost would move them. "They left the room for an hour and all the balls were gone," recounts Meikle in the podcast. "They hadn't been slightly moved or nudged, they were gone."

In the audio recording, the investigators heard a last-minute, hurried effort to remove the balls, and when they unlocked the door, all the balls had vanished. They'd been stashed in an alcove in the wall behind a statue.

Oh, and there are also orange rectangular spots in a hallway of the Dove House that can't be hidden by paint or wallpaper. Anything used to cover them—pictures in frames—are later found broken on the floor. At some point, a guest at the facility was in the hallway looking at the wall and sternly warned an employee that the mysterious spots were a portal to hell and needed to be removed.

Good luck with that.

## APPENDIX A

# THE VAMPYRE

The superstition on which this tale is founded is very general in the East. Among the Arabians it appears to be common: it did not, however, extend itself to the Greeks until after the establishment of Christianity; and it has only assumed its present form since the division of the Latin and Greek churches; at which time, the idea becoming prevalent, that a Latin body could not corrupt if buried in their territory, it gradually increased, and formed the subject of many wonderful stories, still extant, of the dead rising from their graves, and feeding upon the blood of the young and beautiful. In the West it spread, with some slight variation, all over Hungary, Poland, Austria, and Lorraine, where the belief existed, that vampyres nightly imbibed a certain portion of the blood of their victims, who became emaciated, lost their strength, and speedily died of consumptions; whilst these human blood-suckers fattened—and their veins became distended to such a state of repletion, as to cause the blood to flow from all the passages of their bodies, and even from the very pores of their skins.

In the *London Journal* of March 1732 is a curious, and, of course, credible account of a particular case of vampyrism, which is stated to have occurred at Madreyga, in Hungary. It appears, that upon an examination of the commander-in-chief and magistrates of the place, they positively and unanimously affirmed, that, about five years before, a certain Heyduke, named Arnold Paul, had been heard to say, that, at Cassovia, on the frontiers of the Turkish Servia, he had been tormented by a vampyre, but had found a way to rid himself of the evil, by eating some of the earth out of the vampyre's grave, and rubbing himself with his blood. This precaution, however, did not prevent him from becoming a vampyre himself; for, about twenty or thirty days after his death and burial, many persons complained of having been tormented by him, and a deposition was made, that four persons had been deprived of life by his attacks. To prevent further mischief, the inhabitants having consulted their Hadagni, took up the body, and found it (as is supposed to be usual in cases of vampyrism) fresh, and entirely free from corruption, and emitting at the mouth, nose, and ears, pure and florid blood. Proof having been thus obtained, they resorted to the accustomed remedy. A stake was driven entirely through the heart and body of Arnold Paul, at which he is reported to have cried out as dreadfully as if he had been alive. This done, they cut off his head, burned his body, and threw the ashes into his grave. The same measures were adopted with the corses of those persons who had previously died from vampyrism, lest they should, in their turn, become agents upon others who survived them.

Many curious and interesting notices on this singularly horrible superstition might be added; though the present may suffice for the limits of a note, necessarily devoted to explanation, and which may now be concluded by merely remarking, that though the term Vampyre is the one in most general acceptation, there are several others synonymous with it, made use of in various parts of the world: as Vroucolocha, Vardoulacha, Goul [and] Broucoloka.

*The Vampyre; A Tale.* John William Polidori, 1819

# ROUMENIAN SUPERSTITIONS

An approved method for averting the danger of the dwelling being struck by lightning is to form a top by sticking a knife through a piece of bread, and spin it on the floor of the loft during the whole time the storm lasts. The ringing of bells is likewise very efficacious, provided, however, that the bell in question has been cast under a perfectly cloudless sky.

The feast of St. Elias, the 20th of July (August 1), is a very unlucky day, on which the lightning may be expected to strike. If a house struck by lightning begins to burn, it is not allowed to put out the flames, because God has lit the fire and it would be presumption if man were to dare to meddle. In some places it is believed that a fire lit by lightning can only be put out with milk.

Here, as elsewhere, thirteen is an ominous number.

It is bad luck if your path be traversed by a hare, but a fox or wolf crossing your road is a good omen.

Likewise, it is lucky to meet a woman with a jug full of water, while an empty jug is unlucky; therefore, the Roumenian maiden who meets you on the way back from the well will, smiling, display her brimming pitcher as she passes, with a pleased consciousness of bringing good luck; while the girl whose pitcher is empty will slink past shamefacedly, as though she had a crime to conceal.

Every orthodox Roumenian woman is careful to do homage to the water-spirit, the *wodna zena or zona*, which resides in each spring, by spilling a few drops on the ground, after she has emptied her jug. She will never venture to draw the water against the current, for that would strike the spirit home and provoke her anger.

The Roumenian in general avoids the neighbourhood of deep pools of water, especially whirlpools, for here resides the dreadful *balaur*, or the *wodna muz*, the cruel waterman who lies in wait for human victims.

Each forest has likewise its own particular spirit, its *mama padura*, or forest mother. This fairy is in general supposed to be good-natured, especially towards children who have lost their way in the wood. Less to be trusted is *Panusch* (surely a corruption of the Greek god Pan?), who haunts the forest glades and lies in wait for helpless maidens.

The body of a drowned man can only be found again by sticking a lighted candle into a hollowed-out loaf of bread and setting it afloat at night on the river or lake. There where the light comes to a standstill will the corpse be found. Until this has been done the water will continue to rise and the rain to fall.

At the birth of a child each one present takes a stone, and throws it behind him, saying, 'This into the jaws of the Strigoi,' which custom would also seem to suggest Saturn and the swaddled-up stones. As long as the child is unbaptised, it must be carefully watched over, for fear of being changed or otherwise harmed by witch. A piece of iron or a broom laid under its pillow will keep evil charms away.

Even the Roumenian's wedding day is darkened by the shade of superstition. He can never be quite sure of his affection for his bride being a natural, spontaneous feeling, since it may or will have been caused by the evil influence of a witch. Also at church, when the priest offers the blest bread to himself and his new-made wife, he will tremblingly compare the relative sizes of the two pieces, for whoever chances to get the smaller one must inevitably be the first to die.

But nowhere does the inherent superstition of the Roumenian peasant find stronger expression than in his mourning and funeral ceremonies, which are based upon a totally original conception of death.

Among the various omens of approaching death are the ungrounded barking of a dog or the crowing of a black hen. The influence of the latter may, however, be annulled and the catastrophe averted if the bird be put in a sack and carried thrice round the house.

Roots dug up from the churchyard on Good Friday are to be given to people in danger of death. If, however, this and other remedies fail to save the doomed man, then he must have a burning candle put into his hand; for it is considered to be the greatest of all misfortunes if a man die without a candle—a favour the Roumenian durst not refuse to his most deadly enemy.

The corpse must be washed immediately after death, and the dirt, if necessary, scraped off with knives, because the dead man is more likely to find favour with God if he appear before Him in a clean state. Then he is attired in his best clothes, in doing which great care must be taken not to tie anything in a knot, for that would disturb his rest; likewise, he must not be allowed to carry away any particle of iron about his dress (such as buttons, boot nails, &c.), for this would assuredly prevent him from reaching Paradise, the road to which is long, and is, moreover, divided off by several tolls or ferries. To enable the soul to pass through these a piece of money must be laid in the hand, under the pillow, or beneath the tongue of the corpse. In the neighbourhood of Fogaras, where the ferries or toll-bars are supposed to amount to twenty-five, the hair of the defunct is divided into as many plaits, and a piece of money secured in each. Likewise, a small provision of needles, pins, thread, &c., are put into the coffin to enable the pilgrim to repair any damage his clothes may receive on the way.

More decidedly evil, however, is the vampire, or nosferatu, in whom every Roumenian peasant believes as firmly as he does in heaven or hell. There are two sorts of vampires—living and dead. The living vampire is in general the illegitimate offspring of two illegitimate persons, but even a flawless pedigree will not ensure anyone against the intrusion of a vampire into his family vault, since every person killed by a nosferatu becomes likewise a vampire after death, and will continue to suck the blood of other innocent people till the spirit has been exorcised, either by opening the grave of the person suspected and driving a stake through the corpse, or firing a pistol shot into the coffin. In very obstinate cases it is further recommended to cut off the head and replace it in the coffin with the mouth filled with garlic, or to extract the heart and burn it, strewing the ashes over the grave.

Emily Gerard, "Transylvanian Superstitions," *The Nineteenth Century* 18 (July–December 1885): 130–50

# PROFESSOR VAN HELSING GIVES A TEAM PEP TALK, EXPLAINS THE VAMPIRE'S ABILITIES, THE RULES IT FOLLOWS AND GIVES INSTRUCTIONS ON HOW TO KILL IT

[Plot update: In the last few chapters of Bram Stoker's *Dracula*, Dr. Van Helsing is the fearless vampire killer, Mina Harker has been targeted (bitten) by Dracula and is transitioning into a vampire, Johnathan Harker is Mina's husband and was the first to meet Dracula in the vampire's Transylvania castle and Quincey Morris is a rich young Texan who was courting Miss Lucy. But Dracula turned Lucy into a vampire, and Lord Godalming was helping the posse catch "it." Dracula arrived in England at Whitby.]

"There are such beings as vampires; some of us have evidence that they exist. Even had we not the proof of our own unhappy experience, the teachings and the records of the past give proof enough for sane peoples. I admit that at the first I was skeptic. Were it not that through long years I have train myself to keep an open mind, I could not have believe until such time as that fact thunder on my ear. 'See! see! I prove; I prove.' Alas! Had I known at the first what now I know—nay, had I even guess at him—one so precious life had been spared to many of us who did love her. But that is gone; and we must so work, that other poor souls perish not, whilst we can save. The *nosferatu* do not die like the bee when he sting once. He is only stronger; and being stronger, have yet more power to work evil. This vampire which is amongst us is of himself so strong in person as twenty men; he is of cunning more than mortal, for his cunning be the growth of ages; he have still the aids of necromancy, which is, as his etymology imply, the divination by the dead, and all the dead that he can come nigh to are for him at command; he is brute, and more than brute; he is devil in callous, and the heart of him is not; he can, within limitations, appear at will when, and where, and in any of the forms that are to him; he can, within his range, direct the elements; the storm, the fog, the thunder; he can command all the meaner things: the rat, and the owl, and the bat—the moth, and the fox, and the wolf; he can grow and become small; and he can at times vanish and come unknown. How then are we to begin our strike to destroy him? How shall we find his where; and having found it, how can we destroy? My friends, this is much; it is a terrible task that we undertake, and there may be consequence to make the brave shudder. For if we fail in this our fight he must surely win; and then where end we? Life is nothings; I heed him not. But to fail here, is not mere life or death. It is that we become as him; that we henceforward become foul things of the night like him—without heart or conscience, preying on the bodies and the souls of those we love best. To us for ever are the gates of heaven shut; for who shall open them to us again? We go on for all time abhorred by all; a blot on the face of God's sunshine; an arrow in the side of Him who died for man. But we are face to face with duty; and in such case must we shrink? For me, I say, no; but then I am old, and life, with his sunshine, his fair places, his song of birds, his music and his love, lie far behind. You others are young. Some have seen sorrow; but there are fair days yet in store. What say you?"

Whilst he was speaking, Jonathan had taken my hand. I feared, oh so much, that the appalling nature of our danger was overcoming him when I saw his hand stretch out; but it was life to me to feel its touch—so strong, so self-reliant, so resolute. A brave man's hand can speak for itself; it does not even need a woman's love to hear its music.

When the Professor had done speaking my husband looked in my eyes, and I in his; there was no need for speaking between us.

"I answer for Mina and myself," he said.

"Count me in, Professor," said Mr. Quincey Morris, laconically as usual.

"I am with you," said Lord Godalming, "for Lucy's sake, if for no other reason."

Dr. Seward simply nodded. The Professor stood up and, after laying his golden crucifix on the table, held out his hand on either side. I took his right hand, and Lord Godalming his left; Jonathan held my right with his left and stretched across to Mr. Morris. So as we all took hands our solemn compact was made. I felt my heart icy cold, but it did not even occur to me to draw back. We resumed our places, and Dr. Van Helsing went on with a sort of cheerfulness which showed that the serious work had begun. It was to be taken as gravely, and in as businesslike a way, as any other transaction of life:—

"Well, you know what we have to contend against; but we, too, are not without strength. We have on our side power of combination—a power denied to the vampire kind; we have sources of science; we are free to act and think; and the hours of the day and the night are ours equally. In fact, so far as our powers extend, they are unfettered, and we are free to use them. We have self-devotion in a cause, and an end to achieve which is not a selfish one. These things are much.

"Now let us see how far the general powers arrayed against us are restrict, and how the individual cannot. In fine, let us consider the limitations of the vampire in general, and of this one in particular.

"All we have to go upon are traditions and superstitions. These do not at the first appear much, when the matter is one of life and death—nay of more than either life or death. Yet must we be satisfied; in the first place because we have to be—no other means is at our control—and secondly, because, after all, these things—tradition and superstition—are everything. Does not the belief in vampires rest for others—though not, alas! for us— on them? A year ago which of us would have received such a possibility, in the midst of our scientific, sceptical, matter-of-fact nineteenth century? We even scouted a belief that we saw justified under our very eyes. Take it, then, that the vampire, and the belief in his limitations and his cure, rest for the moment on the same base. For, let me tell you, he is known everywhere that men have been. In old Greece, in old Rome; he flourish in Germany all over, in France, in India, even in the Chernosese; and in China, so far from us in all ways, there even is he, and the peoples fear him at this day. He have follow the wake of the berserker Icelander, the devil-begotten Hun, the Slav, the Saxon, the Magyar. So far, then, we have all we may act upon; and let me tell you that very much of the beliefs are justified by what we have seen in our own so unhappy experience. The vampire live on, and cannot die by mere passing of the time; he can flourish when that he can fatten on the blood of the living. Even more, we have seen amongst us that he can even grow younger; that his vital faculties grow strenuous, and seem as though they refresh themselves when his special pabulum is plenty. But he cannot flourish without this diet; he eat not as others. Even friend Jonathan, who lived with him for weeks, did never see him to eat, never! He throws no shadow; he make in the mirror no reflect, as again Jonathan observe. He has the strength of many of his hand—witness again Jonathan when he shut the door against the wolfs, and when he help him from the diligence too. He can transform himself to wolf, as we gather from the ship arrival in Whitby, when he tear open the dog; he can be as bat, as Madam Mina saw him on the window at Whitby, and as friend John saw him fly from this so near house, and as my friend Quincey saw him at the window of Miss Lucy. He can come in mist which he create—that noble ship's captain proved him of this; but, from what we know, the distance he can make this mist is limited, and it can only be round himself. He come on moonlight rays as elemental dust—as again Jonathan saw those sisters in the castle of Dracula. He become so small—we ourselves saw Miss Lucy, ere she was at peace, slip through a hairbreadth space at the tomb door. He can, when once he find his way, come out from anything or into anything, no matter how close it be bound or even fused up with fire—solder you call it. He can see in the dark—no small power this, in a world which is one half shut from the light. Ah, but hear me through. He can do all these things, yet he is not free. Nay; he is even more prisoner than the slave of the galley, than the madman in his cell. He cannot go where he lists; he who is not of nature has yet to obey some of nature's laws—why we know not. He may not enter anywhere at the first, unless there be some one of the household who bid him to come; though afterwards he can come as he please. His power ceases, as does that of all evil things, at the coming of the day. Only at certain times can he have limited freedom. If he be not at the place whither he is bound, he can only change himself at noon or at exact sunrise or sunset. These things are we told, and in this record of ours we have proof by inference. Thus, whereas he can do as he will within his limit, when he have his earth-home, his coffin-home, his hell-home, the place unhallowed, as we saw when he went to the grave of the suicide at Whitby; still at other time he can only change when the time come. It is said, too, that he can only pass running water at the slack or the flood of the tide. Then there are things which so afflict him that he has no power, as the garlic that we know of; and as for things sacred, as this symbol, my crucifix, that was amongst us even now when we resolve, to them he is nothing, but in their presence he take his place far off and silent with respect. There are others, too, which I shall tell you of, lest in our seeking we may need them. The branch of wild rose on his coffin keep him that he move not from it; a sacred bullet fired into the coffin kill him so that he be true dead; and as for the stake through him, we know already of its peace; or the cut-off head that giveth rest. We have seen it with our eyes.

"Thus when we find the habitation of this man-that-was, we can confine him to his coffin and destroy him, if we obey what we know. But he is clever. I have asked my friend Arminius, of Buda-Pesth University, to make his record; and, from all the means that are, he tell me of what he has been. He must, indeed, have been that Voivode Dracula who won his name against the Turk, over the great river on the very frontier of Turkey-land. If it be so, then was he no common man; for in that time, and for centuries after, he was spoken of as the cleverest and the most cunning, as well as the bravest of the sons of the 'land beyond the forest.' That mighty brain and that iron resolution went with him to his grave, and are even now arrayed against us. The Draculas were, says Arminius, a great and noble race, though now and again were scions who were held by their coevals to have had dealings with the Evil One. They learned his secrets in the Scholomance, amongst the mountains over Lake Hermanstadt, where the devil claims the tenth scholar as his due. In the records are such words as 'stregoica'—witch, 'ordog,' and 'pokol'—Satan and hell; and in one manuscript this very Dracula is spoken of as 'wampyr,' which we all understand too well. There have been from the loins of this very one great men and good women, and their graves make sacred the earth where alone this foulness can dwell. For it is not the least of its terrors that this evil thing is rooted deep in all good; in soil barren of holy memories it cannot rest."

*Mina Harker's Journal*, September 30, from Bram Stoker's *Dracula*, 1897

# SCIENTIFIC VIEW OF GHOSTS

The question whether spiritual beings ever become manifest to mankind must always be regarded as one of the deep interest. Few people, perhaps, will readily admit an honest belief in ghosts, but there is, naturally, a disposition to consider eagerly all evidence bearing on their manifestation, and indeed it is probable that under the influence of the midnight hour, with the surroundings supposed to be favorable, all persons find little difficulty in appreciating the possibility of supernatural occurrences.

We therefore find an ever recurring period of discussion of the subject, while an earnest endeavor is now being made to sift the large mass of evidence which is continually forthcoming, in order that any foundation of truth which exists may be discovered.

Secondhand evidence, however—usually the only evidence obtainable—has been brought into deserved contempt in this connection, and notwithstanding the most diligent and patient inquiry, it can scarcely be said to have settled any part of the question to the satisfaction of those whose opinion would be authoritative.

For the love of a good story, savoring of the marvelous, to fear and illusion, to self-deception, exaggeration, and untruth, may be ascribed nine-tenths of the numerous accounts of supernatural occurrences which continually find a ready acceptance, while the failure to obtain trustworthy evidence by those who undertake an honest and scientific investigation would almost cause us to despair of human testimony altogether when it approaches this subject.

There is, however, another method of testing the validity of the belief in supernatural manifestations which it ill surprising is not more often resorted to. We live in an age which has seen and is now seeing a progress in science unparalleled in human history. Every branch of knowledge has been opened and has had new light thrown upon it, and, as the result, we find that many of our older beliefs have had to give way altogether to newer and more rational views, while others have been greatly developed on a surer foundation. The belief in ghosts, originating in times of superstition, and involving certain assumptions with regard to nature and the human senses, can also be examined in the light of our later knowledge, and it may have to stand or fall by the result.

Instead, therefore, of considering the character of witnesses, the confirmation of circumstantial evidence, and the like, let us examine what the statement that a ghost has been seen or manifested can really mean in view of the scientific knowledge of the present day. Let us rather analyze the process of such a manifestation, and the ghostly nature, than question the veracity of the percipient or his sanity.

Modern science will first prove to us that ghosts other than phantoms and hallucinations of the mind can only become manifest to human beings by appearing in some material form. It is certain that nothing can be actually seen or heard except through the medium of the senses, and it would seem to be established that the senses can only respond to outside, or objective, influences in the form of energy acting through matter. Ghosts or spirits, therefore, if they appear to human beings, must for this purpose assume some material form. In order to be seen they must, when analyzed, exist in that form of matter and energy which acts upon the retina of the eye, and in order to be heard they must produce those vibrations of matter which cause the phenomena of sound.

On the other hand, the experiences of those who have seen ghosts would indicate that their material form is by no means substantial. They appear within closed doors without sound or warning, and vanish like the morning mists. Sometimes they affect one of the senses only; at others they are seen, heard, and felt, like ordinary human beings. Yet, in whatever way they are manifested, they must still appear in some material form, and it might be concluded that spiritual beings are able at certain times to give life, as it were, to some form of matter. When the ghost or spirit has accomplished its manifestation, it departs to its spiritual home, and the matter which it had touched into life and energy remains as before, unnoticeable by the ordinary human senses.

Another explanation of such appearances may, however, be suggested. The spiritual manifestation way not depend upon the will of the spirit, upon its power to materialize itself, but rather upon the state of the percipient's mind, and the abnormal development of his senses at the particular time. Spirit and matter are usually opposite terms, but we may nevertheless conceive the so-called spiritual world as in reality a material one analogous to our own. Recent science has shown that there is probably a world of energy and matter hidden from our ordinary senses, of which we can only conjecture from the suggestions obtained when the photographic plate records more than the human eye is ever capable of seeing, or the magnetic needle responds to an influence quite unfelt by our dull senses.

Now it way be that it is in such a hidden world that ghosts have their existence-spirits finding a dwelling place in forms as much material as those of ordinary human beings, but of an essentially different, and perhaps more ethereal, character. Into their bidden world of peculiar and unknown energy mankind cannot usually enter, but at critical times in a one's life, corresponding to the fitful and occasional appearances of ghosts, his senses way be abnormally developed, so that—as with the photographic camera—he sees more than his eye is ordinarily capability of seeing, and may become conscious by sight, or hearing, or touch, of that hidden world in which ghosts live, and move, and have their being. This view would explain much that, on any other ground, is antagonistic to belief in ghosts of any kind. Such difficulties as the perception of the apparition by only one person, or the appearance when the percipient is in an unusual state of mind or health, would be removed, and it must be admitted that the uncertain and fitful character of the visitations, and the failure to occur under any test conditions, would be quite in keeping with such an hypothesis.

These explanations of ghostly phenomena are offered merely as suggestions, which might bring the occurrences into conformity with the ascertained laws of science. It is perhaps doubtful whether the ghostly visitors, who are usually shy with those desirous of becoming well acquainted with them, will not vanish altogether under the critical eye of science, and the belief in them. Born perhaps of the unreasoning state of mind, may not bear any wholesome theory of their existence. There is, however, too strong and sincere a conviction in favor of such a belief for it to be dismissed out of hand. In view of the weighty and prevalent opinion which can be cited in favor of the supernatural manifestations, serious inquiry is greatly to be desired, and some theory of the actual occurrences becomes essential. An endeavor to explain the phenomena scientifically may help to decide the validity of the belief in their existence, or else prevent that unhealthy state of mind which is too often its sole origin.

W.B. Ord, *Scientific American*, July 17, 1897

# PREVENTING THE LOSS OF A SOUL

In some sections of the country it is customary when a death has occurred in the family to cover the mirrors and to keep them shrouded while the body remains in the house. Generally, however, it is only a mirror which happens to be in the room where the body lies which is veiled.

This custom is traced by Professor Fraser in the belief of primitive man—of which belief we still see vestiges remaining—that the ghost, the soul, of a dead person hovers for awhile about its late tenement. A man's reflected image was considered to be part of himself, possibly his "exterior soul"—and concerning the belief in "exterior souls" the professor accumulated a vast amount of data. The idea in veiling the mirror was to obviate the chance of the lingering soul of the deceased taking away with it the "exterior soul" of any person whose reflected image appeared in the glass.

Mirrors are very ancient and before mirrors were introduced there were pieces of bright metal in which an image might be reflected and which were covered upon occasions of death, a custom still observed by some savage tribes.

Whether the "exterior soul" idea applies here, as the professor thinks, or not, it is certain that primitive man like the savage who is the primitive man of today regarded his reflection as something vitally pertaining to his personality, and not was natural that he should protect it against any possibility of contact with a lingering spirit by preventing its existence. And what was begun as a precaution is practiced today because of an atavism which makes the superstitious feel it might be "unlucky" not to do it.

*Lafayette Leader*, October 28, 1927

# SOURCES

## Chapter 1

Conarroe, Carolyn, *Coal Mining in Colorado's Northern Field*. Lafayette, CO: Conarroe Companies, 2001.

————. *Louisville Legends: The Record as History*. Denver, CO: Capitol Hill, 2004.

————. *The Louisville Story*. Louisville, CO: Louisville Times, 1978 and 2000.

Conarroe, Doug, *Lost Lafayette, Colorado*. Charleston, SC: The History Press, 2021.

*Lafayette (CO) Leader*, April 15, 1927.

Leslie B. Kelso Collection 1909–1925 (bulk 1912–1924). BHS 291. Carnegie Library for Local History, Boulder, Colorado.

Morrison, Robyn. "A Small-Town Mayor Challenges Developers." *High Country News* (Paonia, CO), March 31, 2003.

Paddock, Laurence T. "Accidents (Boulder County, Colo.) Chronologies 1884–1929." BHS 328-4-3. Carnegie Library for Local History, Boulder, Colorado.

Rogers, Marie. Oral history interview with Jack and Ruth Davies, interviewed by Rachel Homer, March 10, 1978. OH0012. Carnegie Library for Local History, Boulder, Colorado.

————. Oral history interview with Joe "Cotton" Fletcher and Chelmar "Shine" Miller, interviewed by Marilyn Brand and Charlene Pratt, 1984. OH0861. Carnegie Library for Local History, Boulder, Colorado.

Sedgwick, Icy. "Who Are the Tommyknockers of Cornish Folklore?" Icy Sedgwick, November 23, 2019. icysedgwick.com.

*The X-Files*. Pilot, Season 2, episode 1, September 10, 1993. Planet Claire Quotes. Accessed December 20, 2022. planetclaire.tv/quotes/xfiles/season-one/pilot.

## Chapter 2

Ancestry.com. "Manifest of Alien Passengers for the United States Immigration Office. New York, U.S. 1820–1957." Ancestry.com.

Athenagaia. "The Greek Cross." athenagaia.com.

Auerbach, Nina. *Our Vampires, Ourselves*. Chicago: University of Chicago Press, 1995.

Banes, Melissa. "Harison's Yellow Rose—An Enduring Pioneer." Colorado Mountain Gardens, July 6, 2017. coloradomountaingardener.blogspot.com.

Barry, Krista. "Fact-Checking Folklore: The Lafayette Vampire." Lafayette Historical Society, May 2020.

Boulder County Clerk and Recorder. William A. Nelson deed, 126758.

Boulder County Courts. Probate Records. Colorado State Archives, 1313 Sherman Street, Room 1B-20, Denver, Colorado.

City of Lafayette. Cemetery records and maps from the Lafayette Cemetery archives, 1290 South Public Road, Lafayette, Colorado.

———. "Lafayette Cemetery Records, Lafayette, Boulder County, Colorado." Donated by Nancy Green. March 9, 1999. Municipal Government Reference Collection: Cemeteries, 1973–2005. 749-6-4. Carnegie Library for Local History, Boulder, Colorado.

*Denver Post*. "Epidemic Continues to Rage Thru Italian Section of Denver." November 17, 1918.

Genealogy & Family History. "Instructions for World War I Draft Cards (US)?" October 25, 2012. genealogy.stackexchange.com.

Hutchison, James. *Lafayette, Colorado History: Treeless Plain to Thriving City*. Lafayette, CO: Lafayette Historical Society, 1990.

Hyatt, D. Trent. "How Is Eastern Orthodoxy Different?" Answers in Genesis. April 12, 2017. answersingenesis.org.

Jensen, Jack. Interview with author. 2022 and 2023.

Krishnan, Vidya. *Phantom Plague: How Tuberculosis Shaped History*. New York: Hachette Book Group, 2022.

*Lafayette Leader*. 1918 editions; June 4, 1920; March 6, 1931; October 13, 1933; October 20, 1944.

Lazar, George. Application and employment record, Colorado Fuel and Iron, March 27, 1918. Ancestry.com.

Mathias, "Welchie." Oral history interview, July 2, 1975. Lafayette Public Library. Lafayette, Colorado.

Moloney, Devon. "The Wild Evolution of Vampires, from Bram Stoker to *Dracula Untold*." Wired, October 9, 2014. wired.com.

National Coal & Heritage Trail. 2022. coalheritage.wv.gov.

Pallardy, R. "Vlad the Impaler." *Encyclopedia Britannica*, January 1, 2023. britannica.com.

Pate, Nancy. "Vampires Are Alive and Well in Popular Culture and Gaining Devotees All the Time." *Baltimore Sun*, October 29, 1994.

Peirse, A.L. "Dracula on Film, 1931–1959." In *The Cambridge Companion to "Dracula."* Cambridge, UK: Cambridge University Press, 2017.

Rhodes, Gary. "The First Vampire Films in America." *Nature*, December 21, 2017. nature.com.

*Rocky Mountain News* (Denver, CO), December, 1918.

Starkey, Arun. "The Unerring Influence of Bela Lugosi on Establishing the Goth Subculture." *Far Out*, October 26, 2021. faroutmagazine.co.uk.

Tucker, Abigail. "The Great New England Vampire Panic—Two Hundred Years After the Salem Witch Trials, Farmers Became Convinced That Their Relatives Were Returning from the Grave to Feed on the Living." *Smithsonian Magazine*, October 2012.

U.S. Census. 1910, 1920 and 1930.

Ward, Alie. "Vampirology (Vampires) with Dr. Jeff Holdeman." *Ologies*, October 26, 2022. alieward.com/ologies.

Worland, Rick. "OWI Meets the Monsters: Hollywood Horror Films and War Propaganda, 1942 to 1945." *Cinema Journal* 37, no. 1 (1997): 47–65..

## Chapter 3

Ancestry.com. "1932 R.L. Polk directory of Boulder County." Ancestry.com.

*Annual Report of the Colorado State Inspector of Coal Mines. 1905–1906.* Denver, CO: Smith-Brooks Printing Company, 1907.

Conarroe, Carolyn, *Coal Mining in Colorado's Northern Field.* Lafayette, CO: Conarroe Companies, 2001.

———. *Louisville Legends: The Record as History.* Denver, CO: Capitol Hill, 2004.

———. *The Louisville Story.* Louisville, CO: Louisville Times, 1978 and 2000.

*Lafayette (CO) Leader*, September 26, 1924.

*Louisville (CO) Times*, July 9, 1936.

## Chapter 4

Fernández-Poncela, Anna M. "Las niñas buenas van al cielo y las malas…Género y narrativa oral tradicional, Nueva Sociedad." *Fundación Friedrich Ebert* 135 (1999): 104–15.

*Louisville (CO) Times*, July 22, 1995.

Romero, Mike. "City of Lafayette—Mike Romero," *Lafayette News*, July 22, 1995.

Shaw Beatty, Judith. *La Llorona: Encounters with the Weeping Woman.* N.p.: self-published, 2020.

Walraven, Ed. "Evidence for a Developing Variant of 'La Llorona.'" *Western Folklore*, April 1991.

## Chapter 5

Bacon, Bridget. "City of Louisville, 740 Front Street History." Louisville Historical Museum, May 2012.

Conarroe, Doug. "History Lost: Louisville's Historic Hecla Casino Razed by Balfour Senior Living." Lafayette History, January 30, 2018. www.lafayettehistory.com.

*Daily Camera* (Boulder, CO), February 14, 1918 and March 15, 1935.

Estop, Richard. "Investigation: Old Louisville Inn." Boulder County Paranormal Research Society, 2008. coloradoparanormal.tripod.com.

Foster, Cliff. "Land Was Industrial," *Louisville (CO) Times*, April 17, 1985.

*Longmont (CO) Ledger*, April 9, 1909, and August 20, 1909.

*Louisville (C)O) Times*, December 30, 1955, and August 19, 1998.

## Chapter 6

Hutchison, James. *Lafayette, Colorado History: Treeless Plain to Thriving City*. Lafayette, CO: Lafayette Historical Society, 1990.

Meikle, Olivia. "Old Town Haunted History Tour." *What's Her Name*, October 2020. whatshernamepodcast.com.

"Public Road Intensive Level Survey of Lafayette, Colorado, 1998." Architectural Inventory Form, Resource 5BL11232. Bunyak Research Associates, Littleton, Colorado.

# INDEX

# ABOUT THE AUTHOR

Doug Conarroe is a fourth-generation Coloradan who grew up in Louisville, Colorado. His parents, Percy and Carolyn Conarroe, owned and operated the *Louisville Times*, *Lafayette News* and *Erie Review* from 1965 to 1997. Doug was the editor of those newspapers in the 1990s and later joined the *Denver Post*. He has a journalism degree and an MBA from the University of Colorado and published the *North Forty News* from 2011 to 2017. His previous books include *80026: An Illustrated History of Lafayette, Colorado* and *Lost Lafayette, Colorado*. Doug's local history blog is at lafayettehistory.com. He and his wife, Dana Coffield, have lived in Lafayette since 1995.